Better Homes and Gardens

all-time-favorite
Crockery
cooker recipes

Better Homes and Gardens® Books
Des Moines, Iowa

Better Homes and Gardens® Books
An imprint of Meredith® Books

all-time-favorite Crockery cooker recipes
Editor: Lisa Holderness
Contributing Editors: Carrie Holcomb Mills, Spectrum Communication Services, Inc.
Art Director: Conyers Design Inc.
Designer: Sundie Ruppert
Photographers: Peter Krumhardt, Scott Little
Food Stylists: Lynn Blanchard, Janet Pittman
Illustrator: Chad Johnston
Copy and Production Editor: Terri Fredrickson
Contributing Proofreaders: Gretchen Kauffman, Susan J. Kling
Electronic Production Coordinator: Paula Forest
Editorial and Design Assistants: Judy Bailey, Mary Lee Gavin, Karen Schirm
Test Kitchen Director: Lynn Blanchard
Production Manager: Pam Kvitne, Marjorie J. Schenkelberg

Meredith® Books
Editor in Chief: James D. Blume
Design Director: Matt Strelecki
Managing Editor: Gregory H. Kayko
Executive Food Editor: Jennifer Dorland Darling

Director, Retail Sales and Marketing: Terry Unsworth
Director, Sales, Special Markets: Rita McMullen
Director, Sales, Premiums: Michael A. Peterson
Director, Sales, Retail: Tom Wierzbicki
Director, Book Marketing: Brad Elmitt
Director, Operations: George A. Susral
Director, Production: Douglas M. Johnston

Vice President, General Manager: Jamie L. Martin

Better Homes and Gardens® Magazine
Editor in Chief: Jean LemMon
Executive Food Editor: Nancy Byal

Meredith Publishing Group
President, Publishing Group: Stephen M. Lacy
Vice President, Finance and Administration: Max Runciman

Meredith Corporation
Chairman and Chief Executive Officer: William T. Kerr

Chairman of the Executive Committee: E. T. Meredith III

All of us at Better Homes and Gardens® Books are dedicated to providing you with the information and ideas you need to create delicious foods. We welcome your comments and suggestions. Write to us at:

Better Homes and Gardens® Books
Cookbook Editorial Department
1716 Locust St.
Des Moines, IA 50309-3023

If you would like to purchase any of our books, check wherever quality books are sold. Visit our website at bhg.com

Our seal assures you that every recipe in *all-time-favorite Crockery cooker recipes* has been tested in the Better Homes and Gardens® Test Kitchen. This means that each recipe is practical and reliable, and meets our high standards of taste appeal. We guarantee your satisfaction with this book for as long as you own it.

Shown on the cover:
White Bean-Spinach Soup
(see recipe, page 8)

introduction

Busy schedules make our lives hectic and leave each of us looking for ways to make our day a little easier. The crockery cooker is one appliance that helps to simplify cooking and make our favorite dishes more feasible.

Whether you're working full-time or in the home, running errands or preparing to entertain guests, the crockery cooker virtually eliminates the last-minute panic of mealtime preparation. By choosing the low-heat or high-heat setting, you can adjust the cooker to your meal schedule and have every meal ready when you are.

all-time-favorite Crockery cooker recipes is brimming with 80 recipes for everything from soups to snacks. Plus, you'll find basic guidelines and tips for using your cooker. So relax—and serve a delicious crockery cooker dish tonight.

contents

crockery cooker basics

No one has to convince you of the ease of using a crockery cooker. It's a busy family's answer to getting meals on the table easily. With an exciting array of flavors and ingredients, the recipes contained in this cookbook will inspire and tantalize you. But before you start cooking, these tips will help you get the most from your cooker.

Know Your Crockery Cooker

There are two types of cookers:

Continuous slow cooker. All recipes in this book were tested in this type of cooker, which continuously cooks foods slowly at a very low wattage. The heating coils, or elements, wrap around the sides of the cooker and remain on continuously. This type of cooker has fixed settings: low (about 200°), high (about 300°), and in some models, automatic (shifts from high to low heat automatically). The ceramic liner may or may not be removable.

Intermittent cooker. This type of cooker is not recommended for the recipes in this cookbook. The heating element or coil is located below the food container and cycles on and off during operation. If your cooker has a dial indicating temperatures in degrees, you'll know that this is the type of cooker you have. Because the recipes in this book need continuous slow cooking temperatures, this type of cooker will not cook the food properly.

What Size Do I Need?

Crockery cookers can range in size from 1 to 6 quarts. The recipes in this book specify the recommended size to use. Check the capacity of your cooker to see whether it fits the recommendation in the recipe.

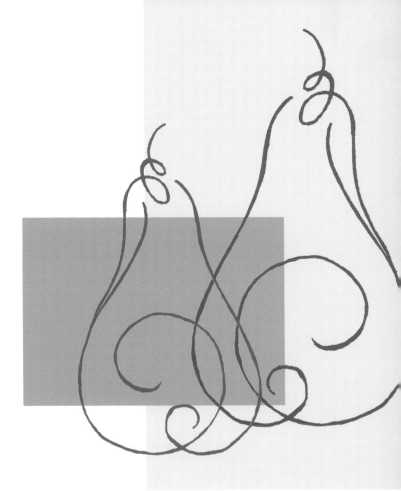

Fuss-Free Cooking

If you want dinner to cook all day, use the low-heat setting of your cooker. This allows most foods to cook from 10 to 12 hours. For a shorter cooking time, use the high-heat setting, which cooks most foods in 3 to 6 hours (depending on the recipe). Cooking times may vary depending on the cooker, but our timings generally will work with all continuous slow cookers. Note: When a recipe recommends only cooking on one setting, do not use the other setting because your recipe may not turn out properly.

Keep Food Safe

For food safety reasons, remove cooked food from the crockery cooker before storing it. If you store the warm food and the crockery liner in the refrigerator, the food may not cool down quickly enough. Cooling foods quickly is the key to keeping foods safe from bacteria. Place leftovers in a storage container and refrigerate or freeze.

Crockery Cooking with Dairy Products

Dairy products, such as milk, cream, and natural cheeses, will break down from extended cooking. Utilize substitutes such as reconstituted condensed soups and nonfat dry milk powder. You also can use evaporated milk, if you add it during the last 30 to 60 minutes of cooking time. Stir natural cheese into the finished dish just before serving.

Trimming the Fat

To keep finished dishes low in fat, remove skin from poultry or all visible fat from meats. When browning meats, spray a skillet with nonstick coating or, if oil is needed, use as little as possible. When testing these recipes, the Better Home and Gardens® Test Kitchen found that many meats didn't need browning. However, chicken tended to "slough," causing clear, broth-based recipes to cloud. Therefore, some chicken recipes require browning.

Crockery Cooker Care

To clean the cooker's ceramic liner, use a soft cloth and warm soapy water (or wash removable ceramic liners in a dishwasher). Avoid using abrasive cleaners and cleansing pads. Never immerse the cooker or the cord in water.

Spicy Pork and Potato Stew
(see recipe, page 20)

soups, chilis, & stews

white bean-spinach soup

Tuscan cuisine influences this earthy soup, with white beans. Tomatoes and deep green spinach add Provençal freshness. Serve with hearty Italian bread. (Recipe pictured on the front cover.)

2 15-ounce cans white kidney (cannellini) beans, rinsed and drained

1 medium onion, chopped

2 cloves garlic, minced

1½ teaspoons snipped fresh marjoram or ½ teaspoon dried marjoram, crushed

2 14½-ounce cans reduced-sodium chicken broth (3½ cups)

4 cups fresh spinach or kale, coarsely chopped (about 5 ounces)

1 cup seeded and coarsely chopped plum tomatoes (3 or 4 tomatoes)

tips from the kitchen

the right thyme
Timing is everything when it comes to adding herbs during cooking. If you use a dried herb, add it at the beginning of cooking. If you use a fresh herb, add it at the end of cooking so it doesn't lose all of its flavor and color during the long cooking time. Fresh rosemary is an exception, as it can withstand long cooking times.

In a 3½-, 4-, or 5-quart crockery cooker place beans, onion, garlic, and dried marjoram (if using). Pour chicken broth over all.

Cover; cook on low-heat setting for 8 to 10 hours or on high-heat setting for 4 to 5 hours. Stir in spinach and tomatoes; stir in fresh marjoram (if using). Cover; cook about 5 minutes more or until spinach is tender. Season to taste with pepper. Makes 5 servings.

Nutrition facts per serving: 138 calories, 13 g protein, 29 g carbohydrate, 2 g total fat (0 g saturated), 0 mg cholesterol, 751 mg sodium

White Bean-Spinach Soup with Sausage:
Prepare as at left, except prick 12 ounces fresh mild Italian sausage links with a fork. In large skillet combine sausage and ¼ cup water. Bring to boiling; reduce heat. Simmer, covered, about 15 minutes or until sausage is no longer pink. Remove sausage; cut into ¼- to ⅜-inch-thick slices. Place sausage slices on top of vegetables in cooker. Proceed as at left.

Nutrition facts per serving: 305 calories, 23 g protein, 31 g carbohydrate, 14 g total fat (5 g saturated), 39 mg cholesterol, 1,196 mg sodium

beef 'n' brew vegetable soup

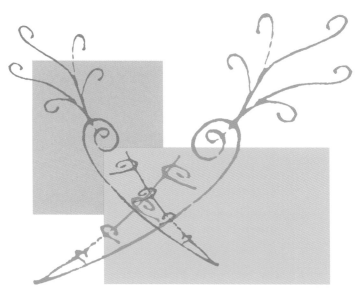

3 medium onions, sliced

1 pound carrots, cut into ¹/₂-inch-thick slices

4 parsnips, cut into ¹/₂-inch-thick slices

4 cloves garlic, minced

2 bay leaves

1 tablespoon snipped fresh thyme or 1 teaspoon dried thyme, crushed

¹/₂ teaspoon pepper

2 tablespoons quick-cooking tapioca

1¹/₂ pounds beef stew meat, cut into 1-inch cubes

1 14¹/₂-ounce can beef broth (1³/₄ cups)

1 12-ounce can beer

In a 5- or 6-quart crockery cooker place onions, carrots, parsnips, garlic, bay leaves, dried thyme (if using), and pepper. Sprinkle with tapioca. Place meat on top of vegetables. Pour beef broth and beer over all.

Cover; cook on low-heat setting for 10 to 12 hours or on high-heat setting for 5 to 6 hours. To serve, remove bay leaves; stir in fresh thyme (if using). Makes 6 servings.

Nutrition facts per serving: 354 calories, 31 g protein, 35 g carbohydrate, 9 g total fat (3 g saturated), 82 mg cholesterol, 336 mg sodium

zesty beef and vegetable soup

Soup lovers can't resist this combination of beef and vegetables in a spicy tomato base. Complete the meal with corn bread and honey.

1 pound ground beef

1/2 cup chopped onion

2 cloves garlic, minced

2 cups packaged shredded cabbage with carrot (coleslaw mix)

1 10-ounce package frozen whole kernel corn

1 9-ounce package frozen cut green beans

4 cups hot-style vegetable juice

1 14½-ounce can Italian-style stewed tomatoes

2 tablespoons Worcestershire sauce

1 teaspoon dried basil, crushed

1/4 teaspoon pepper

In a large skillet cook ground beef, onion, and garlic until meat is brown. Drain off fat.

In a 3½-, 4-, or 5-quart crockery cooker combine meat mixture, coleslaw mix, frozen corn, frozen beans, vegetable juice, undrained tomatoes, Worcestershire sauce, basil, and pepper.

Cover; cook on low-heat setting for 8 to 10 hours or on high-heat setting for 4 to 5 hours. Makes 6 servings.

Nutrition facts per serving: 269 calories, 19 g protein, 29 g carbohydrate, 10 g total fat (4 g saturated), 48 mg cholesterol, 925 mg sodium

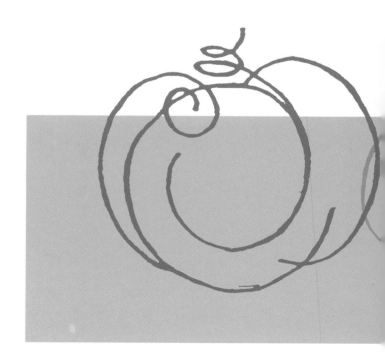

quick vegetable-beef soup

This full-flavored soup uses just a few easy-to-find ingredients.

1 pound ground beef

1 14½-ounce can beef broth (1¾ cups)

1¼ cups water

1 10-ounce package frozen mixed
   vegetables

1 14½-ounce can tomatoes, cut up

1 11⅛-ounce can condensed tomato soup
   with Italian herbs

1 tablespoon dried minced onion

¼ teaspoon garlic powder

In a large skillet cook beef until brown. Drain off fat.

Transfer meat to a 3½- or 4-quart crockery cooker. Add beef broth, water, and frozen vegetables. Add undrained tomatoes, tomato soup, onion, and garlic powder.

Cover; cook on low-heat setting for 7 to 8 hours or on high-heat setting for 3½ to 4 hours. Makes 4 to 6 servings.

Nutrition facts per serving: 360 calories, 25 g protein, 28 g carbohydrate, 17 g total fat (6 g saturated), 71 mg cholesterol, 1,118 mg sodium

calico ham and bean soup

Try a pound of purchased bean mix or a pound of any one of the beans for this soup. For thicker soup, mash part of the beans before serving.

½ cup dry navy or Great Northern beans

½ cup dry black beans or kidney beans

½ cup dry lima beans

½ cup dry garbanzo beans

½ cup dry green split peas

6 cups water

2 cups fully cooked ham cut into ½-inch pieces (about 10 ounces)

1 cup chopped onion

1 cup chopped carrot

1 teaspoon dried basil, crushed

1 teaspoon dried oregano, crushed

¾ teaspoon salt

¼ teaspoon pepper

2 bay leaves

6 cups water

Rinse beans and peas: drain. In a large saucepan combine the beans, peas, and 6 cups water. Bring to boiling; reduce heat. Simmer, uncovered, for 10 minutes. Drain and rinse beans and peas.

Meanwhile, in a 3½-, 4-, or 5-quart crockery cooker combine ham, onion, carrot, basil, oregano, salt, pepper, and bay leaves. Stir in drained beans, peas, and 6 cups fresh water.

Cover; cook on low-heat setting for 8 to 10 hours or on high-heat setting for 4 to 5 hours. Discard the bay leaves. Season to taste with additional salt and pepper. Makes 8 servings.

Nutrition facts per serving: 244 calories, 19 g protein, 36 g carbohydrate, 3 g total fat (1 g saturated), 11 mg cholesterol, 696 mg sodium

curried split pea soup

A Christmas ham glazed with curried cranberries inspired this flavorful soup.

1 pound dry green split peas, rinsed and drained

1 1-pound meaty ham bone or 1 pound smoked pork hocks

1½ cups cubed ham

1½ cups chopped celery

1 cup chopped onion

1 cup chopped carrot

⅓ cup dried cranberries

2 bay leaves

4 teaspoons curry powder

1 tablespoon dried marjoram, crushed

¼ teaspoon pepper

6 cups water

In a 3½- or 4-quart crockery cooker combine the split peas, ham bone or smoked pork hocks, ham, celery, onion, carrot, cranberries, bay leaves, curry powder, marjoram, and pepper. Add water. Cover and cook on low-heat setting for 10 to 12 hours or on high-heat setting for 5 to 6 hours.

Remove ham bone or pork hocks from crockery cooker. Remove meat from bone; discard bone. Chop meat and return to soup. Discard the bay leaves. Makes 6 servings.

Nutrition facts per serving: 376 calories, 29 g protein, 58 g carbohydrate, 4 g total fat (1 g saturated), 25 mg cholesterol, 626 mg sodium

chicken and vegetable bean soup

This hearty recipe also tastes great without the chicken.

1	cup dry Great Northern beans
6	cups water
1	cup chopped onion
1	medium fennel bulb, trimmed and cut into $\frac{1}{2}$-inch pieces
2	medium carrots, chopped
2	cloves garlic, minced
2	tablespoons snipped fresh parsley
1	teaspoon dried thyme, crushed
1	teaspoon dried marjoram, crushed
$\frac{1}{4}$	teaspoon pepper
$4\frac{1}{2}$	cups chicken broth
$2\frac{1}{2}$	cups chopped cooked chicken
1	$14\frac{1}{2}$-ounce can stewed tomatoes

Rinse beans; drain. In a large saucepan combine beans and the 6 cups water. Bring to boiling; reduce heat. Simmer, uncovered, for 2 minutes. Remove from heat. Cover and let stand for 1 hour. (Or, skip the boiling step and soak beans overnight in a covered pan.) Drain and rinse beans.

Meanwhile, in a $3\frac{1}{2}$-, 4-, or 5-quart crockery cooker combine onion, fennel, carrots, garlic, parsley, thyme, marjoram, and pepper. Place beans on top of vegetables. Pour chicken broth over all.

Cover; cook on low-heat setting for 8 to 10 hours or on high-heat setting for 4 to 5 hours.

If using low-heat setting, turn to high-heat setting. Stir in chicken and undrained tomatoes. Cover and cook on high-heat setting for 30 minutes longer or until heated through. Makes 4 to 6 servings.

Nutrition facts per serving: 471 calories, 44 g protein, 46 g carbohydrate, 13 g total fat (3 g saturated), 74 mg cholesterol, 1,250 mg sodium

deviled chicken soup

"Deviled" refers to a food that is seasoned with piquant ingredients such as red pepper, hot pepper sauce, or, as in this dish, mustard. Add more or less to your liking.

1 pound skinless, boneless chicken thighs

1 large red potato, chopped

1/2 of a 16-ounce package (1 1/2 cups) frozen whole kernel corn

1 medium onion, chopped

1/2 cup chopped celery

3 tablespoons Dijon-style mustard

1/4 teaspoon pepper

1/8 teaspoon garlic powder

2 1/2 cups vegetable juice

1 14 1/2-ounce can reduced-sodium chicken broth (1 3/4 cups)

tips from the kitchen

cutting vegetables to size Vegetables intended for the crockery cooker are cut into bite-size pieces not only for the convenience in eating, but for better cooking, too. Some vegetables can take longer to cook than meat in crockery cookers. By cutting the vegetables into small pieces (and, if using large cuts of meat, placing the meat on top of the vegetables), you can be sure the vegetables will be tender and ready to eat when the meat is done.

Rinse chicken; pat dry. Cut into bite-size pieces.

In a 3 1/2-, 4-, or 5-quart crockery cooker combine the chicken, potato, corn, onion, celery, mustard, pepper, and garlic powder. Pour vegetable juice and chicken broth over all.

Cover; cook on low-heat setting for 8 to 10 hours or on high-heat setting for 4 to 5 hours. Makes 6 servings.

Nutrition facts per serving: 192 calories, 15 g protein, 23 g carbohydrate, 5 g total fat (1 g saturated), 36 mg cholesterol, 800 mg sodium

lentil-tortellini soup

Lentils, ham or Canadian-style bacon, and cheese-filled tortellini make this soup a hearty meal in itself. Warm breadsticks are all you need to round it out.

1/2 cup dry lentils

2 cups coarsely shredded carrots

1 large onion, finely chopped

4 ounces chopped cooked ham or Canadian-style bacon

2 cloves garlic, minced

2 tablespoons snipped fresh basil or 2 teaspoons dried basil, crushed

1 1/2 tablespoons snipped fresh thyme or 1 1/2 teaspoons dried thyme, crushed

1/4 teaspoon pepper

5 cups reduced-sodium chicken broth

1 cup water

1 9-ounce package refrigerated cheese-filled tortellini

4 cups torn fresh spinach

Rinse lentils; drain. Place lentils in a 3½-, 4-, or 5-quart crockery cooker. Add the carrots, onion, ham or Canadian-style bacon, garlic, dried basil and thyme (if using), and pepper. Pour broth and water over all.

Cover; cook on low-heat setting for 6½ to 7 hours or on high-heat setting for 3¼ to 3½ hours. If using low-heat setting, turn to high-heat setting. Stir in tortellini. Cover and cook on high-heat setting 30 minutes longer. To serve, stir in spinach and the fresh basil and thyme (if using). Makes 6 servings.

Nutrition facts per serving: 245 calories, 16 g protein, 35 g carbohydrate, 5 g total fat (1 g saturated), 30 mg cholesterol, 1,023 mg sodium

spicy southwestern beef stew

1 pound beef chuck pot roast

1 tablespoon cooking oil

2 14½-ounce cans Mexican-style stewed tomatoes

1½ cups coarsely chopped onion

1 15-ounce can jalapeño pinto beans or pinto beans

3½ cups beef broth

1 6-ounce can tomato paste

4 teaspoons chili powder

1 tablespoon dried Italian seasoning, crushed

½ teaspoon crushed red pepper

¼ teaspoon ground cloves

¼ teaspoon ground allspice

¼ teaspoon ground cinnamon

1 medium zucchini, halved lengthwise and cut into ½-inch-thick pieces

1 medium yellow or green sweet pepper, cut into 1-inch pieces

Trim fat from meat. Cut meat into 1-inch cubes. In a large skillet brown meat, half at a time, in hot oil. Drain off fat.

Transfer meat to a 3½-, 4-, or 5-quart crockery cooker. Add undrained tomatoes, onion, and beans.

In a medium bowl combine beef broth, tomato paste, chili powder, Italian seasoning, crushed red pepper, cloves, allspice, and cinnamon. Add to cooker.

Cover; cook on low-heat setting for 10 to 12 hours or on high-heat setting for 5 to 6 hours.

If using low-heat setting, turn to high-heat setting. Add zucchini and sweet peppers. Cover and cook on high-heat setting 30 minutes longer. Makes 6 servings.

Nutrition facts per serving: 360 calories, 35 g protein, 35 g carbohydrate, 10 g total fat (3 g saturated), 76 mg cholesterol, 1,258 mg sodium

ginger and molasses beef stew

Ginger, molasses, and raisins give this highly flavored stew a pleasant sweetness. Pair the stew with a salad of mixed greens, grapes, and toasted walnuts.

2 pounds lean beef stew meat, cut into 1-inch cubes

1 tablespoon cooking oil

4 carrots, sliced

2 medium parsnips, sliced

1 large onion, sliced

1 stalk celery, sliced

1 1¼-inch-thick slice fresh ginger or ½ teaspoon ground ginger

¼ cup quick-cooking tapioca

1 14½-ounce can diced tomatoes

¼ cup vinegar

¼ cup molasses

1 teaspoon salt

½ teaspoon pepper

½ cup raisins

In a large skillet brown meat, a third at a time, in hot oil. Drain off fat.

In a 3½-, 4-, or 5-quart crockery cooker place carrots, parsnips, onion, celery, and fresh ginger (if using). Sprinkle tapioca over vegetables. Add meat. Combine undrained tomatoes, vinegar, molasses, salt, pepper, and ground ginger (if using); pour over meat.

Cover; cook on low-heat setting for 9 to 10 hours or on high-heat setting for 4 to 5 hours. Stir in raisins; cover and cook for 30 minutes longer. To serve, remove slice of fresh ginger (if using) before serving. Makes 8 servings.

Nutrition facts per serving: 564 calories, 40 g protein, 58 g carbohydrate, 19 g total fat (5 g saturated), 110 mg cholesterol, 962 mg sodium

beef and cider stew

Simple ingredients add up to a wonderful wintertime stew. Apples and apple cider lend a subtle sweet flavor while thyme adds a minty-lemon touch.

1 pound beef stew meat, cut into 1-inch cubes

1 tablespoon cooking oil

4 carrots or parsnips, chopped

2 medium red-skinned potatoes, chopped

2 onions, halved and sliced

2 small apples, cored and cut into ½-inch pieces

1 stalk celery, chopped

2 tablespoons quick-cooking tapioca

1 cup apple cider

1 cup water

2 teaspoons instant beef bouillon granules

1 teaspoon snipped fresh thyme or ¼ teaspoon dried thyme, crushed

¼ teaspoon pepper

In a large skillet brown meat, half at a time, in hot oil. Drain off fat.

Place carrots or parsnips, potatoes, onions, apples, and celery in a 3½-, 4-, or 5-quart crockery cooker. Sprinkle tapioca over vegetables. Add meat. In a medium bowl combine the cider, water, bouillon granules, dried thyme (if using), and pepper; pour over meat.

Cover; cook on low-heat setting for 8 to 10 hours or on high-heat setting for 4 to 5 hours. Stir in fresh thyme (if using). Makes 6 servings.

Nutrition facts per serving: 289 calories, 21 g protein, 34 g carbohydrate, 8 g total fat (2 g saturated), 55 mg cholesterol, 372 mg sodium

spicy pork and potato stew

Long, deep green poblano peppers are mild to medium-hot and have an irregular sweet-pepper shape. Remove the membranes and seeds for the mildest flavor. (Recipe pictured on pages 6–7.)

1 pound boneless pork shoulder roast, cut into 1-inch cubes

1 tablespoon cooking oil

1 pound whole, tiny new potatoes, quartered

2 medium onions, chopped

2 fresh poblano peppers, seeded and cut into 1-inch pieces (see tip, page 23)

1 fresh jalapeño pepper, seeded and chopped (see tip, page 23)

4 cloves garlic, minced

2 inches stick cinnamon

3 cups chicken broth

1 14½-ounce can diced tomatoes

1 tablespoon chili powder

1 teaspoon dried oregano, crushed

¼ teaspoon black pepper

¼ cup snipped fresh cilantro or parsley

Hot cooked basmati or long-grain rice (optional)

In a large skillet brown meat, half at a time, in hot oil. Drain off fat.

Place potatoes, onions, poblano peppers, jalapeño pepper, garlic, and stick cinnamon in a 3½- or 4-quart crockery cooker. Add meat. In a medium bowl combine chicken broth, undrained tomatoes, chili powder, oregano, and black pepper; pour over all.

Cover; cook on low-heat setting for 8 to 10 hours or on high-heat setting for 4 to 5 hours. Discard stick cinnamon. Stir in cilantro or parsley. If desired, serve stew over hot cooked rice. Makes 6 servings.

Nutrition facts per serving: 285 calories, 19 g protein, 28 g carbohydrate, 11 g total fat (3 g saturated), 50 mg cholesterol, 753 mg sodium

moroccan lamb and fruit stew

Richly seasoned cubes of meat slow-cook with dried fruits in this hearty stew. Serve it over couscous—tiny flakes of semolina found in the pasta section of your supermarket.

1 to 2 teaspoons crushed red pepper

³/₄ teaspoon ground turmeric

³/₄ teaspoon ground ginger

³/₄ teaspoon ground cinnamon

¹/₂ teaspoon salt

2 pounds boneless leg of lamb or beef bottom round roast, well trimmed and cut into 1- to 1¹/₂-inch pieces

2 tablespoons olive oil or cooking oil

2 large onions, chopped

3 cloves garlic, minced

1 14¹/₂-ounce can beef broth (1³/₄ cups)

1 tablespoon cornstarch

2 tablespoons cold water

1 cup pitted dates

1 cup dried apricots

Hot cooked couscous or rice

¹/₄ cup slivered almonds, toasted

In a shallow mixing bowl combine crushed red pepper, turmeric, ginger, cinnamon, and salt. Coat meat with seasoning mixture. In a large skillet brown meat, a third at a time, in hot oil.

Transfer meat to a 3¹/₂- or 4-quart crockery cooker. Add onions and garlic; stir to combine. Pour beef broth over all. Cover and cook on low-heat setting for 7 to 9 hours or on high-heat setting for 3¹/₂ to 4¹/₂ hours.

Skim fat from surface of the juices in the crockery cooker. Stir cornstarch into cold water; stir into crockery cooker. Add dates and apricots; stir to combine. If using low-heat setting, turn to high-heat setting. Cover and cook on high-heat setting 30 minutes longer or until mixture is slightly thickened and bubbly.

To serve, spoon stew over hot couscous or rice. Top with almonds. Makes 6 to 8 servings.

Nutrition facts per serving: 550 calories, 34 g protein, 75 g carbohydrate, 14 g total fat (3 g saturated), 76 mg cholesterol, 475 mg sodium

chili with double bean toss

A two-bean salad makes this chili stand out from the rest. This lime-garlic-dressed salad adds a refreshing complement to the hearty chili soup.

1   pound boneless beef top round steak

1   tablespoon cooking oil

2   14½-ounce cans diced tomatoes

1   14½-ounce can beef broth (1¾ cups)

1   large onion, chopped

1   or 2 fresh jalapeño or serrano peppers, finely chopped (see tip, page 23)

2   cloves garlic, minced

2   tablespoons cornmeal

4   teaspoons chili powder

1   tablespoon brown sugar

1½ teaspoons dried oregano, crushed

½   teaspoon ground cumin

¼   teaspoon black pepper

1   recipe Double Bean Toss

    Dairy sour cream (optional)

Trim fat from meat. Thinly slice meat across the grain into bite-size pieces. In a large skillet brown meat, half at a time, in hot oil. Drain off fat.

In a 3½- or 4-quart crockery cooker combine undrained tomatoes, beef broth, onion, jalapeño or serrano peppers, garlic, cornmeal, chili powder, brown sugar, oregano, cumin, and black pepper. Stir in meat.

Cover; cook on low-heat setting for 10 to 12 hours or on high-heat setting for 5 to 6 hours. Serve chili in bowls with Double Bean Toss as a side dish. If desired, top with sour cream. Makes 6 servings.

Double Bean Toss: In a medium bowl combine one 15-ounce can pinto beans and one 15-ounce can black beans, rinsed and drained. Add ½ teaspoon finely shredded lime peel, 1 tablespoon lime juice, 1 tablespoon salad oil, and 1 clove garlic, minced. Toss to mix.

Nutrition facts per serving: 315 calories, 28 g protein, 33 g carbohydrate, 9 g total fat (2 g saturated), 48 mg cholesterol, 1,049 mg sodium

hearty beef chili

For a fall open house, serve this meat-filled chili. Offer several toppers—such as olives, tortilla chips, or sour cream—so guests can personalize their chili.

1   29-ounce can tomatoes, cut up

1   10-ounce can chopped tomatoes and green chile peppers

2   cups vegetable juice or tomato juice

1   to 2 tablespoons chili powder

1   teaspoon ground cumin

1   teaspoon dried oregano, crushed

3   cloves garlic, minced

1½   pounds beef or pork stew meat, cut into 1-inch cubes

2   cups chopped onion

1½   cups chopped celery

1   cup chopped green sweet pepper

2   15-ounce cans black, kidney, and/or garbanzo beans, drained and rinsed

Toppers, such as shredded Mexican cheese or cheddar cheese, dairy sour cream, thinly sliced green onion, snipped fresh cilantro, thinly sliced fresh jalapeño peppers, and/or sliced pitted ripe olives (optional)

In a 6-quart crockery cooker combine both cans of undrained tomatoes, vegetable or tomato juice, chili powder, cumin, oregano, and garlic. Stir in the meat, onion, celery, and sweet pepper.

Cover; cook on low-heat setting for 8 to 10 hours or on high-heat setting for 4 to 5 hours. If using low-heat setting, turn to high-heat setting. Stir in the beans; cover and cook on high-heat setting 15 minutes longer. Spoon into bowls. If desired, serve with toppers. Makes 10 servings.

Nutrition facts per serving: 224 calories, 24 g protein, 24 g carbohydrate, 6 g total fat (2 g saturated), 49 mg cholesterol, 807 mg sodium

tips from the kitchen

chile pepper pointers *Fresh chile peppers contain pungent oils (the membranes and the seeds carry the heat). To protect your hands when handling fresh chile peppers, wear plastic gloves or put plastic bags over your hands. Always wash your hands and nails thoroughly in hot, soapy water after handling chile peppers.*

tex-mex chili

For a less spicy chili, omit the chopped jalapeño peppers and use regular vegetable juice.

1	pound bulk pork sausage or ground beef
2	cloves garlic, minced
3	to 4 teaspoons chili powder
¹/₂	teaspoon ground cumin
1	15¹/₂-ounce can red kidney beans, rinsed and drained
1	cup chopped celery
1	cup chopped onion
¹/₂	cup chopped green sweet pepper
1	to 2 fresh jalapeño peppers, chopped (see tip, page 23)
1	14¹/₂-ounce can tomatoes, cut up
1	10-ounce can chopped tomatoes with green chile peppers
1	cup hot-style vegetable juice or hot-style tomato juice
1	6-ounce can tomato paste
¹/₄	teaspoon salt
	Shredded cheddar cheese
	Dairy sour cream

In a large skillet cook the sausage or beef and garlic until meat is brown. Drain off fat. Stir in chili powder and cumin; cook 2 minutes more.

Meanwhile, in a 3¹/₂-, 4-, or 5-quart crockery cooker combine beans, celery, onion, sweet pepper, and jalapeño peppers. Add both cans of undrained tomatoes, vegetable juice or tomato juice, tomato paste, and salt. Stir in meat mixture.

Cover; cook on low-heat setting for 8 to 10 hours or on high-heat setting for 4 to 5 hours. Ladle chili into soup bowls. Pass shredded cheese and sour cream with chili. Makes 4 to 6 servings.

Nutrition facts per serving: 477 calories, 26 g protein, 44 g carbohydrate, 25 g total fat (11 g saturated), 66 mg cholesterol, 2,012 mg sodium

white chili

For the cooked chicken, poach three or four skinned and boned chicken breast halves in boiling water, covered, about 12 minutes or until no pink remains. Drain chicken, cool slightly, and then chop.

3 15-ounce cans Great Northern, pinto, or white kidney (cannellini) beans, rinsed and drained

2½ cups chopped cooked chicken

1 cup chopped onion

1½ cups chopped red, green, and/or yellow sweet pepper

2 fresh jalapeño peppers, chopped (see tip, page 23)

2 cloves garlic, minced

2 teaspoons ground cumin

½ teaspoon salt

½ teaspoon dried oregano, crushed

3½ cups chicken broth

Shredded Monterey Jack cheese (optional)

Broken tortilla chips (optional)

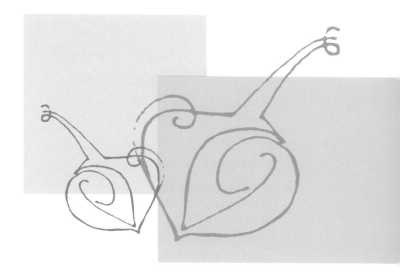

In a 3½-, 4-, or 5-quart crockery cooker combine the drained beans, chicken, onion, sweet pepper, jalapeño peppers, garlic, cumin, salt, and oregano. Stir in the chicken broth.

Cover; cook on low-heat setting for 8 to 10 hours or on high-heat setting for 4 to 5 hours.

Ladle the soup into bowls. If desired, top each serving with some cheese and tortilla chips. Makes 8 servings.

Nutrition facts per serving: 310 calories, 28 g protein, 38 g carbohydrate, 5 g total fat (1 g saturated), 43 mg cholesterol, 523 mg sodium

easy cassoulet

This streamlined, healthful version of the classic French dish features chicken thighs and smoked turkey sausage.

8 ounces skinless, boneless chicken thighs

2 medium carrots, cut into 1/2-inch pieces

1 medium red or green sweet pepper, cut into 1/2-inch pieces

1 cup chopped onion

3 cloves garlic, minced

2 15-ounce cans white kidney (cannellini) beans or Great Northern beans, rinsed and drained

1 14 1/2-ounce can Italian-style stewed tomatoes

8 ounces fully cooked smoked turkey sausage, halved lengthwise and cut into 1/2-inch-thick slices

1 1/2 cups chicken broth

1/2 cup dry white wine or chicken broth

1 tablespoon snipped fresh parsley

1 teaspoon dried thyme, crushed

1/4 teaspoon ground red pepper

1 bay leaf

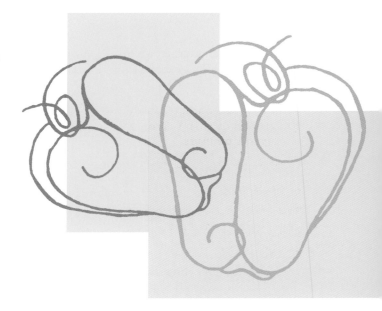

Rinse chicken; pat dry. Cut chicken into 1-inch pieces.

Place carrots, sweet pepper, onion, and garlic in a 3½-, 4-, or 5-quart crockery cooker. Top with beans, undrained tomatoes, sausage, and chicken.

In a medium bowl combine chicken broth, wine, parsley, thyme, red pepper, and bay leaf. Add to cooker.

Cover; cook on low-heat setting for 7 to 8 hours or on high-heat setting for 3½ to 4 hours. Discard bay leaf. Makes 6 servings.

Nutrition facts per serving: 259 calories, 22 g protein, 31 g carbohydrate, 7 g total fat (2 g saturated), 44 mg cholesterol, 974 mg sodium

corn and sausage chowder

Slow cooking brings out the sausage flavor of this creamy, hearty soup.

1 pound fully cooked smoked turkey sausage, halved lengthwise and cut into 1/2-inch-thick slices

3 cups loose-pack frozen hash brown potatoes with onions and sweet peppers

1 medium carrot, coarsely chopped

1 stalk celery, coarsely chopped

2 10³/₄-ounce cans condensed golden corn soup

2¹/₂ cups water

Snipped fresh chives or parsley

Place sausage, frozen hash brown potatoes, carrot, and celery in a 3½-, 4-, or 5-quart crockery cooker. In a medium bowl combine soup and water. Add to cooker.

Cover; cook on low-heat setting for 8 to 10 hours or on high-heat setting for 4 to 5 hours. Ladle into bowls. Sprinkle with chives or parsley. Makes 6 servings.

Nutrition facts per serving: 275 calories, 16 g protein, 32 g carbohydrate, 8 g total fat (1 g saturated), 52 mg cholesterol, 668 mg sodium

tips from the kitchen

cooking under cover *Because a crockery cooker cooks food at a low temperature, removing the lid can reduce the interior temperature inside the cooker dramatically. Therefore, when you lift the cover to stir or add ingredients, replace the lid as quickly as possible, especially when cooking on the low-heat setting. An uncovered cooker can lose up to 20 degrees of cooking heat in as little as 2 minutes. A quick peek, however, will change the temperature by only 1 or 2 degrees. So to keep the temperature constant, resist lifting the lid. If you have no reason to peek—don't!*

mexican chicken chowder

Sour cream adds a creamy richness to this flavor-packed chowder.

2½ cups chopped cooked chicken

1 11-ounce can whole kernel corn with sweet peppers, drained

1 10¾-ounce can condensed cream of potato soup

1 4-ounce can diced green chile peppers

2 tablespoons snipped fresh cilantro

1 1¼-ounce envelope taco seasoning mix

3 cups chicken broth

1 8-ounce carton dairy sour cream

½ of an 8-ounce package cheese spread with jalapeño peppers, cubed

In a 3½- or 4-quart crockery cooker combine chicken, corn, soup, undrained chile peppers, cilantro, and taco seasoning mix. Stir in chicken broth.

Cover; cook on low-heat setting for 8 to 10 hours or on high-heat setting for 4 to 5 hours.

Stir about 1 cup of the hot soup into sour cream. Stir sour cream mixture and cheese into the mixture in crockery cooker; cover and let stand 5 minutes. Stir until combined. Makes 6 servings.

Nutrition facts per serving: 376 calories, 30 g protein, 21 g carbohydrate, 21 g total fat (10 g saturated), 93 mg cholesterol, 1,986 mg sodium

manhattan clam chowder

2 6½-ounce cans minced clams

2 cups peeled potatoes, cut into ½-inch cubes

1 cup chopped onion

1 cup chopped celery with leaves

½ cup chopped green sweet pepper

1 14½-ounce can Italian-style stewed tomatoes

1½ cups hot-style tomato juice or hot-style vegetable juice

½ teaspoon salt

½ teaspoon dried thyme, crushed

1 bay leaf

4 slices bacon, crisp-cooked, drained, and crumbled

Drain clams, reserving liquid. Cover clams; chill.

In a 3½- or 4-quart crockery cooker combine reserved clam liquid, potatoes, onion, celery, green sweet pepper, undrained tomatoes, tomato juice or vegetable juice, salt, thyme, and bay leaf.

Cover; cook on low-heat setting for 8 to 10 hours or on high-heat setting for 4 to 5 hours.

If using low-heat setting, turn to high-heat setting. Stir in clams. Cover and cook on high-heat setting 5 minutes. Discard bay leaf. Ladle soup into bowls. Sprinkle each serving with crumbled bacon. Makes 6 servings.

Nutrition facts per serving: 146 calories, 9 g protein, 24 g carbohydrate, 3 g total fat (1 g saturated), 42 mg cholesterol, 761 mg sodium

brunswick fish chowder

Adding the fish partially frozen keeps it from overcooking. And, if you're watching your sodium intake, use sodium-reduced soups and broths available at your grocery store.

1	pound frozen cod or whiting fillets
2	medium potatoes, finely chopped
1	cup chopped onion
2	cloves garlic, minced
1	10³/₄-ounce can condensed cream of celery soup
1	10-ounce package frozen whole kernel corn
1	10-ounce package frozen baby lima beans
1¹/₂	cups chicken broth
¹/₃	cup dry white wine or water
1	teaspoon lemon-pepper seasoning
1	bay leaf
1	14¹/₂-ounce can stewed tomatoes
¹/₃	cup nonfat dry milk powder

Let fish stand at room temperature while preparing other ingredients.

In a 3½-, 4-, or 5-quart crockery cooker combine potatoes, onion, garlic, soup, frozen corn, frozen lima beans, chicken broth, white wine or water, lemon-pepper seasoning, and bay leaf. Halve the fillets crosswise; place frozen fish fillet halves in the cooker.

Cover; cook on low-heat setting for 7 to 8 hours or on high-heat setting for 3½ to 4 hours.

Discard bay leaf. Break fish into bite-size chunks with a fork. Stir in undrained tomatoes and dry milk powder. Makes 6 servings.

Nutrition facts per serving: 300 calories, 23 g protein, 44 g carbohydrate, 4 g total fat (1 g saturated), 37 mg cholesterol, 1,058 mg sodium

black bean and corn soup

When cooking dried beans, adding acidic foods such as tomatoes slows down the cooking process. That's why the tomatoes are stirred into this soup just before serving.

2¼ cups dry black beans (1 pound)

1 10-ounce package frozen whole kernel corn

1 cup chopped onion

4 cloves garlic, minced

1 tablespoon ground cumin

1 teaspoon salt

1 teaspoon ground coriander

¼ to ½ teaspoon bottled hot pepper sauce

4 cups boiling water

1 14½-ounce can Mexican-style stewed tomatoes

1 recipe Pepper Salsa

Rinse beans; place in a large saucepan. Add enough water to cover beans by 2 inches. Bring to boiling; reduce heat. Simmer, uncovered, for 10 minutes. Remove from heat. Cover; let stand for 1 hour. (Or, skip the boiling step and soak beans overnight in a covered pan.) Drain and rinse beans.

In a 3½-, 4-, or 5-quart crockery cooker combine the beans, corn, onion, garlic, cumin, salt, coriander, and hot pepper sauce. Pour boiling water over all.

Cover; cook on low-heat setting for 8 to 10 hours or on high-heat setting for 4 to 5 hours. To serve, mash beans slightly to thicken soup. Stir in tomatoes. Serve with Pepper Salsa. Makes 6 servings.

Pepper Salsa: In a medium bowl combine 1½ cups finely chopped yellow and/or green sweet peppers; 1 small fresh jalapeño pepper, finely chopped (see tip, page 23); ⅓ cup chopped, seeded tomato; and 1 tablespoon snipped fresh cilantro. Cover and chill for up to 24 hours.

Nutrition facts per serving: 321 calories, 18 g protein, 62 g carbohydrate, 2 g total fat (0 g saturated), 0 mg cholesterol, 604 mg sodium

Swiss Steak
(see recipe, page 34)

meat-filled main dishes

swiss steak

Beef round steak slowly simmers in an herbed tomato sauce in this crockery cooker version of a family favorite. (Recipe pictured on pages 32-33.)

1   pound boneless beef round steak, cut ³/₄ inch thick

1   tablespoon cooking oil

1   small onion, sliced and separated into rings

1   stalk celery, sliced

1   medium carrot, sliced

2   tablespoons quick-cooking tapioca

¹/₂   teaspoon dried thyme, crushed

¹/₄   teaspoon salt

¹/₄   teaspoon pepper

1   14¹/₂-ounce can tomatoes, cut up

    Hot cooked rice or noodles

Trim fat from meat. Cut meat into 4 portions. In large skillet brown meat on both sides in hot oil. Drain off fat.

Place onion, celery, and carrot in a 3½- or 4-quart crockery cooker. Sprinkle with tapioca, thyme, salt, and pepper. Pour undrained tomatoes over vegetables. Top with meat.

Cover and cook on low-heat setting for 10 to 12 hours. Skim off fat. Serve with rice or noodles. Makes 4 servings.

Nutrition facts per serving: 352 calories, 31 g protein, 34 g carbohydrate, 9 g total fat (2 g saturated), 72 mg cholesterol, 404 mg sodium

south-of-the-border steak and beans

This chili-spiced mixture is served over rice for a one-dish dinner that will please Mexican-food fanatics. Use instant rice to keep last-minute prep to a minimum.

1½ pounds beef flank steak

1 10-ounce can chopped tomatoes with green chile peppers

1 medium onion, chopped

2 cloves garlic, minced

1 tablespoon snipped fresh oregano or 1 teaspoon dried oregano, crushed

1 teaspoon chili powder

1 teaspoon ground cumin

¼ teaspoon salt

¼ teaspoon black pepper

2 small green, red, and/or yellow sweet peppers, cut into strips

1 15-ounce can pinto beans, rinsed and drained

Hot cooked rice

Crumbled queso fresco* or feta cheese (optional)

Snipped fresh oregano (optional)

Trim fat from meat. Place meat in a 3½- or 4-quart crockery cooker. In a bowl stir together undrained tomatoes, onion, garlic, dried oregano (if using), chili powder, cumin, salt, and black pepper. Pour over meat.

Cover; cook on low-heat setting for 7 to 9 hours or on high-heat setting for 3½ to 4½ hours.

If using low-heat setting, turn to high-heat setting. Add sweet pepper strips and pinto beans. Cover and cook on high-heat setting 30 minutes more. Remove meat; cool slightly. Shred or thinly slice meat across the grain. Stir fresh oregano (if using) into bean mixture.

To serve, spoon rice into soup bowls. Arrange meat on top of rice. Spoon bean mixture over meat. If desired, sprinkle with cheese and additional oregano. Makes 6 servings.

*Note: Queso fresco (KAY-so FRESK-o), meaning "fresh cheese" in Spanish, can be found in stores specializing in Mexican food products.

Nutrition facts per serving: 345 calories, 28 g protein, 37 g carbohydrate, 9 g total fat (4 g saturated), 53 mg cholesterol, 642 mg sodium

italian steak rolls

Thin beef round steak is rolled around a savory vegetable filling to make these hearty steak rolls.

1½ to 2 pounds boneless beef round steak

½ cup grated carrot

⅓ cup chopped zucchini

⅓ cup chopped red or green sweet pepper

¼ cup sliced green onions

2 tablespoons grated Parmesan cheese

1 tablespoon snipped fresh parsley

1 clove garlic, minced

¼ teaspoon black pepper

1 tablespoon cooking oil

1 14-ounce jar meatless spaghetti sauce

Hot cooked pasta

Trim fat from meat. Cut meat into 6 portions. Place the meat between 2 pieces of plastic wrap and, with a meat mallet, pound steak to a ⅛- to ¼-inch thickness.

In a small bowl combine carrot, zucchini, sweet pepper, green onions, Parmesan cheese, parsley, garlic, and black pepper. Spoon one-sixth of the vegetable mixture onto each piece of meat. Roll up meat around the filling and tie each roll with string or secure with wooden toothpicks.

In large skillet brown meat rolls on all sides in hot oil. Transfer meat rolls to a 3½- or 4-quart crockery cooker. Pour spaghetti sauce over the meat rolls.

Cover; cook on low-heat setting for 7 to 8 hours or on high-heat setting for 3½ to 4 hours. Discard string or toothpicks. Serve meat rolls with hot cooked pasta. Makes 6 servings.

Nutrition facts per serving: 358 calories, 33 g protein, 32 g carbohydrate, 10 g total fat (3 g saturated), 74 mg cholesterol, 341 mg sodium

pot roast with basil mashed potatoes

What could be more comforting on a chilly day than a hearty, melt-in-your-mouth pot roast? Mashed potatoes combined with fresh basil add a special touch.

2 carrots, cut into ½-inch pieces

1 medium turnip, peeled and cubed (1 cup)

1 small onion, chopped

½ cup snipped dried tomatoes (not oil-packed)

1 clove garlic, minced

1 teaspoon instant beef bouillon granules

½ teaspoon dried basil, crushed

½ teaspoon dried oregano, crushed

⅛ teaspoon pepper

1 1½- to 2-pound boneless beef chuck pot roast

1 cup water

1 10-ounce package frozen lima beans or whole kernel corn

1 cup frozen peas

1 20-ounce package refrigerated mashed potatoes

1 tablespoon finely snipped fresh basil

In a 3½- or 4-quart crockery cooker combine the carrots, turnip, onion, dried tomatoes, garlic, bouillon granules, dried basil, dried oregano, and pepper. Trim fat from meat. If necessary, cut roast to fit into cooker; reserve trimmings for another use. Place meat on top of vegetables. Pour water over all.

Cover; cook on low-heat setting for 8 to 10 hours or on high-heat setting for 4 to 5 hours. Stir in the lima beans or corn and peas. Let stand, covered, for 10 minutes.

Meanwhile, prepare mashed potatoes according to package directions, except stir the fresh basil into potatoes just before serving. Remove meat and vegetables from cooker with a slotted spoon. If desired, reserve cooking juices. Serve meat and vegetables over hot mashed potatoes. If desired, serve cooking juices over meat. Makes 6 servings.

Nutrition facts per serving: 436 calories, 35 g protein, 46 g carbohydrate, 12 g total fat (5 g saturated), 87 mg cholesterol, 497 mg sodium

bavarian beef

This German-style pot roast gains tenderness and flavor as it cooks while you're away from home.

1 2½- to 3-pound boneless beef chuck
   pot roast

1 tablespoon cooking oil

2 cups sliced carrot

2 cups chopped onions

1 cup sliced celery

¾ cup chopped kosher-style dill pickles

½ cup dry red wine or beef broth

⅓ cup German-style mustard

½ teaspoon coarse ground black pepper

¼ teaspoon ground cloves

2 bay leaves

2 tablespoons all-purpose flour

2 tablespoons dry red wine or beef broth

Hot cooked spaetzle or noodles

Chopped kosher-style dill pickle
   (optional)

Crumbled cooked bacon (optional)

Trim fat from roast. If necessary, cut roast to fit into a 3½- or 4-quart crockery cooker; reserve trimmings for another use.

In a large skillet brown the roast slowly on all sides in hot oil. Drain off fat.

Place the carrots, onions, celery, and ¾ cup pickles in 3½- or 4-quart crockery cooker. Place the meat on top of the vegetables. In a small bowl combine the red wine or beef broth, mustard, pepper, cloves, and bay leaves. Pour over meat. Cover and cook on low-heat setting for 8 to 10 hours or on high-heat setting for 4 to 5 hours. Remove the meat from the cooker and place on a serving platter; keep warm.

For gravy, transfer vegetables and cooking liquid to a 2-quart saucepan. Skim off fat. Discard bay leaves. Stir together flour and the 2 tablespoons wine or beef broth. Stir into the mixture in saucepan. Cook and stir over medium heat until thickened and bubbly. Cook and stir for 1 minute more. Serve meat and vegetables with gravy and hot cooked spaetzle or noodles. If desired, top with additional chopped pickle and bacon. Makes 8 servings.

Nutrition facts per serving: 454 calories, 41 g protein, 35 g carbohydrate, 15 g total fat (5 g saturated), 158 mg cholesterol, 548 mg sodium

harvest dinner

A touch of cinnamon seasons this old-fashioned dinner favorite. If you prefer, skip the gravy and spoon the juices over the beef.

1 1½- to 2-pound boneless beef chuck pot roast

1 tablespoon cooking oil

1 medium onion, sliced

4 medium sweet potatoes, peeled and quartered (1¼ pounds)

¾ cup water

1½ teaspoons instant beef bouillon granules

¼ teaspoon celery seed

¼ teaspoon ground cinnamon

¼ teaspoon pepper

2 tablespoons cornstarch (optional)

2 tablespoons cold water (optional)

Apple wedges (optional)

Trim fat from roast. If necessary, cut roast to fit into a 3½- or 4-quart crockery cooker; reserve trimmings for another use. In a large skillet brown roast on all sides in hot oil. Drain off fat.

Place onion, then sweet potatoes into a 3½- or 4-quart crockery cooker. Place meat on top of vegetables.

In a small bowl combine water, bouillon granules, celery seed, cinnamon, and pepper. Pour over meat and vegetables.

Cover; cook on low-heat setting for 8 to 10 hours or on high-heat setting for 4 to 5 hours.

Remove meat and vegetables from cooker and place on platter; reserve juices. Skim fat from juices. Pass juices. (Or, if desired, for gravy, pour juices into glass measuring cup. If necessary, add water to make 2 cups juice. In a saucepan stir cornstarch into 2 tablespoons cold water; add juices. Cook and stir until thickened and bubbly. Cook and stir 2 minutes more. Serve gravy with roast and vegetables.) If desired, garnish platter with apple wedges. Makes 6 servings.

Nutrition facts per serving: 328 calories, 30 g protein, 30 g carbohydrate, 10 g total fat (3 g saturated), 82 mg cholesterol, 282 mg sodium

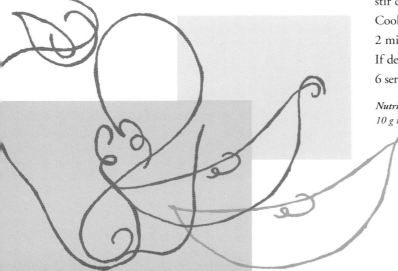

spiced beef brisket

For a real time-saver, freeze half of this plentiful main course. Put the frozen portion in the refrigerator to thaw the night before, and it'll be ready to reheat for dinner on a busy day.

1   3¹/₂- to 4-pound fresh beef brisket

2   cups water

¹/₄   cup catsup

1   envelope regular onion soup mix

2   tablespoons Worcestershire sauce

1   clove garlic, minced

¹/₂   teaspoon ground cinnamon

¹/₄   teaspoon pepper

¹/₄   cup cold water

4   teaspoons all-purpose flour

Trim fat from brisket. If necessary, cut brisket to fit into a 3½- or 4-quart crockery cooker; reserve trimmings for another use. Place brisket in cooker.

In a medium bowl combine the 2 cups water, catsup, soup mix, Worcestershire sauce, garlic, cinnamon, and pepper. Pour over brisket.

Cover; cook on low-heat setting for 8 to 10 hours.

Remove beef; keep warm. Pour juices into a glass measuring cup. Skim off fat. Transfer ¾ cup of the liquid to a moisture- and vapor-proof container. Cool slightly. Seal, label, and freeze for up to 6 months. For gravy, in a small saucepan stir the ¼ cup cold water into the flour. Stir in another ¾ cup cooking liquid. Cook and stir until thickened and bubbly. Cook and stir 1 minute more.

Slice beef thinly across the grain. Transfer half of the beef to a moisture- and vapor-proof container. Seal, label, and freeze for up to 6 months. Serve remaining beef with the hot gravy. Makes 2 meals (5 or 6 servings each).

Note: To serve frozen meat portion, thaw meat and cooking liquid. Warm meat in a covered baking dish in a 350° oven for 20 minutes. For gravy, in a small saucepan stir together the ¾ cup cooking liquid, ¼ cup cold water, and 4 teaspoons all-purpose flour. Cook and stir until thickened and bubbly. Cook and stir 1 minute more.

Nutrition facts per serving: 310 calories, 35 g protein, 6 g carbohydrate, 15 g total fat (5 g saturated), 110 mg cholesterol, 575 mg sodium

beef stroganoff

This slow-cooked version of the classic features tender chunks of beef in a rich herbed sauce ladled over noodles or rice.

1½ pounds beef stew meat, cut into
      1-inch cubes

1 tablespoon cooking oil

2 cups sliced fresh mushrooms

½ cup sliced green onions

2 cloves garlic, minced

½ teaspoon dried oregano, crushed

¼ teaspoon salt

¼ teaspoon dried thyme, crushed

¼ teaspoon pepper

1 bay leaf

1½ cups beef broth

⅓ cup dry sherry

1 8-ounce carton dairy sour cream

½ cup all-purpose flour

¼ cup water

Hot cooked noodles or rice

Snipped fresh parsley (optional)

In a large skillet brown beef, half at a time, in hot oil. Drain off fat.

In a 3½-quart crockery cooker combine beef, mushrooms, green onions, garlic, oregano, salt, thyme, pepper, and bay leaf. Pour beef broth and sherry over all.

Cover; cook on low-heat setting for 8 to 10 hours or on high-heat setting for 4 to 5 hours. Discard bay leaf.

If using low-heat setting, turn to high-heat setting. Mix together sour cream, flour, and water. Stir about 1 cup of the hot liquid into sour cream mixture. Return all to cooker; stir to combine. Cover and cook on high-heat setting for 30 minutes or until thickened and bubbly.

Serve over hot cooked noodles or rice. If desired, sprinkle with snipped fresh parsley. Makes 6 servings.

Nutrition facts per serving: 497 calories, 36 g protein, 38 g carbohydrate, 20 g total fat (9 g saturated), 135 mg cholesterol, 368 mg sodium

herbed mushroom round steak

Bottom round steak—less expensive than top round steak—is a good choice for the crockery cooker because the moist-heat cooking tenderizes the meat.

2 pounds beef round steak, cut ¾ inch thick

1 tablespoon cooking oil

1 medium onion, sliced

2 cups sliced fresh mushrooms or two 4½-ounce jars sliced mushrooms

1 10¾-ounce can condensed cream of mushroom soup

¼ cup dry white wine (optional)

½ teaspoon dried oregano, crushed

¼ teaspoon dried thyme, crushed

¼ teaspoon pepper

Hot cooked noodles

Trim fat from meat. Cut meat into 6 portions. In large skillet brown meat on both sides in hot oil. Drain off fat.

Place onion slices and mushrooms in a 3½- or 4-quart crockery cooker. Place meat on top of vegetables.

In a small bowl combine soup, wine (if desired), oregano, thyme, and pepper; pour over meat.

Cover; cook on low-heat setting for 8 to 10 hours or on high-heat setting for 4 to 5 hours. Serve over hot cooked noodles. Makes 6 servings.

Nutrition facts per serving: 414 calories, 42 g protein, 27 g carbohydrate, 15 g total fat (4 g saturated), 123 mg cholesterol, 488 mg sodium

italian-style meat loaf

Getting meat loaf into and out of the cooker is a snap when you use foil strips as "handles."

1 8-ounce can pizza sauce

1 beaten egg

½ cup chopped onion

½ cup chopped green sweet pepper

⅓ cup fine dry seasoned bread crumbs

½ teaspoon garlic salt

¼ teaspoon black pepper

¼ teaspoon fennel seed, crushed (optional)

1½ pounds lean ground beef

½ cup shredded mozzarella cheese (2 ounces)

tips from the kitchen

toting foods safely
Crockery cooked foods are great to tote to a picnic or party. To tote, after the food is completely cooked, wrap the cooker in heavy foil, several layers of newspaper, or a heavy towel. Then place the cooker in an insulated container. The food should stay hot for up to 2 hours (do not hold for longer). If there is electricity at your picnic or party site, plug in the cooker. The food will stay warm for hours on the low-heat setting.

Reserve ⅓ cup pizza sauce; cover and chill. In a medium bowl combine remaining pizza sauce and egg. Stir in onion, green sweet pepper, bread crumbs, garlic salt, black pepper, and fennel (if desired). Add ground beef and mix well.

Crisscross three 18×2-inch foil strips (place on a sheet of waxed paper to keep counter clean). In center of the foil strips shape a 6-inch round meat loaf. Bringing up foil strips, lift and transfer meat and foil to a 3½-, 4-, or 5-quart crockery cooker. Press meat away from sides of the cooker to avoid burning.

Cover and cook on low-heat setting for 7 to 9 hours or on high-heat setting for 3½ to 4½ hours (or to 170° internal temperature).

Spread meat with the reserved pizza sauce. Sprinkle with mozzarella cheese. Cover cooker and let stand 5 to 10 minutes.

Using foil strips, carefully lift meat loaf and transfer to a serving plate; discard the foil strips. Makes 8 servings.

Nutrition facts per serving: 228 calories, 20 g protein, 8 g carbohydrate, 13 g total fat (5 g saturated), 83 mg cholesterol, 510 mg sodium

pork chops and mustard-sauced potatoes

6 pork loin chops, cut ¾ inch thick

1 tablespoon cooking oil

1 10¾-ounce can condensed cream of mushroom soup

¼ cup dry white wine or chicken broth

¼ cup Dijon-style mustard

1 teaspoon dried thyme, crushed

1 clove garlic, minced

¼ teaspoon pepper

6 medium potatoes, cut into ¼-inch-thick slices

1 medium onion, sliced

In a large skillet brown pork chops on both sides, half at a time, in hot oil. Drain off fat.

In a large bowl combine soup, wine or chicken broth, mustard, thyme, garlic, and pepper. Add potatoes and onion, stirring to coat. Transfer to a 3½- or 4-quart crockery cooker. Place chops on top of potatoes.

Cover; cook on low-heat setting for 7 to 8 hours or on high-heat setting for 3½ hours. Makes 6 servings.

Nutrition facts per serving: 335 calories, 17 g protein, 39 g carbohydrate, 11 g total fat (3 g saturated), 39 mg cholesterol, 705 mg sodium

orange-herbed pork roast

Serve this delicately seasoned roast with parslied new potatoes and steamed baby carrots.

1 2½- to 3-pound pork sirloin roast

½ teaspoon garlic powder

½ teaspoon ground ginger

½ teaspoon dried thyme, crushed

¼ teaspoon pepper

1 tablespoon cooking oil

1 cup chicken broth

2 tablespoons sugar

2 tablespoons lemon juice

2 teaspoons soy sauce

1½ teaspoons finely shredded orange peel

3 tablespoons cornstarch

½ cup orange juice

Trim fat from pork roast. If necessary, cut roast to fit into a 3½-, 4-, or 5-quart crockery cooker; reserve trimmings for another use. In a small bowl combine garlic powder, ginger, thyme, and pepper. Rub spice mixture over entire surface of meat with fingers. In a large skillet brown roast slowly on all sides in hot oil. Drain off fat.

Transfer meat to 3½-, 4-, or 5-quart crockery cooker. Combine chicken broth, sugar, lemon juice, soy sauce, and orange peel; pour over roast.

Cover; cook on low-heat setting for 8 to 10 hours or on high-heat setting for 4 to 5 hours.

Transfer roast to a serving platter; keep warm. For sauce, pour juices into glass measuring cup. Skim off fat. Measure 2 cups liquid (if necessary, add water to make 2 cups). Transfer to saucepan. Stir cornstarch into orange juice; stir into juices in saucepan. Cook and stir until thickened and bubbly. Cook and stir 2 minutes more. Season to taste with salt and pepper. Pass sauce with meat. Makes 8 servings.

Nutrition facts per serving: 197 calories, 29 g protein, 8 g carbohydrate, 6 g total fat (2 g saturated), 78 mg cholesterol, 224 mg sodium

cranberry-raspberry-sauced pork chops

Hot cooked couscous complements this company-special entrée made from simple ingredients.

6 boneless smoked pork chops

1 cup cranberry-orange sauce

1/2 cup seedless red raspberry preserves

1 teaspoon quick-cooking tapioca

1 teaspoon finely shredded lemon peel

1/4 teaspoon ground cardamom

3 fresh apricots or plums, pitted and sliced

Hot cooked couscous

Place pork chops in a 3½- or 4-quart crockery cooker.

For sauce, in a small bowl combine cranberry-orange sauce, raspberry preserves, tapioca, lemon peel, and cardamom. Pour over chops.

Cover; cook on low-heat setting for 7 to 8 hours or on high-heat setting for 3½ to 4 hours. Stir in sliced fruit. Cover; let stand 5 minutes. Serve with hot cooked couscous. Makes 6 servings.

Nutrition facts per serving: 340 calories, 23 g protein, 50 g carbohydrate, 5 g total fat (1 g saturated), 27 mg cholesterol, 1,040 mg sodium

tips from the kitchen

safety tips Always remember to unplug your cooker before cleaning and never immerse the cooker or cord in water. Also, to avoid cracking the crockery insert, add only warm water if the unit is still hot.

ribs with apples and sauerkraut

Quick browning in a skillet seals in natural juices, adding flavor and aroma to the pork country-style ribs.

2½   pounds pork country-style ribs, cut crosswise in half and cut into 1- or 2-rib portions

1   tablespoon cooking oil

2   medium potatoes, sliced ½ inch thick

2   medium carrots, sliced ¼ inch thick

1   medium onion, thinly sliced

1   8-ounce can sauerkraut, rinsed and drained

½   cup apple cider or apple juice

2   teaspoons caraway or fennel seed

⅛   teaspoon ground cloves

2   tablespoons cold water

1   tablespoon all-purpose flour

½   of a large apple, cored and thinly sliced

1   tablespoon snipped fresh parsley

In a large skillet brown pork ribs on both sides in hot oil over medium-high heat.

Place potatoes, carrots, onion, browned pork ribs, and sauerkraut in a 3½- or 4-quart crockery cooker. In small bowl combine apple cider or juice, caraway seed, and cloves. Pour over sauerkraut.

Cover; cook on low-heat setting for 8 to 10 hours or on high-heat setting for 4 to 5 hours.

Remove meat and vegetables to a serving platter, reserving the juices in the crockery cooker. Keep meat and vegetables warm.

For gravy, strain juices into a glass measuring cup. Skim off fat. Measure 1 cup juices (if necessary, add water to make 1 cup); pour into a small saucepan. In a small bowl stir cold water into flour. Stir into the juices in saucepan. Cook and stir until thickened and bubbly. Stir in the apple. Cook and stir for 1 minute more or until heated through. If desired, season to taste with salt and pepper. Stir in parsley just before serving. Serve gravy with ribs and vegetables. Makes 4 servings.

Nutrition facts per serving: 431 calories, 31 g protein, 32 g carbohydrate, 20 g total fat (7 g saturated), 103 mg cholesterol, 371 mg sodium

tomato-sauced pork ribs

There are no bones about it. These boneless pork ribs, cooked in a rich tomato sauce, make perfect partners for a mound of hot noodles. Grab extra napkins!

1	28-ounce can crushed tomatoes
2	stalks celery, chopped
1	medium green sweet pepper, chopped
1	medium onion, chopped
2	tablespoons quick-cooking tapioca
1½	teaspoons sugar
1½	teaspoons snipped fresh basil or ½ teaspoon dried basil, crushed
½	teaspoon salt
¼	teaspoon black pepper
¼	teaspoon bottled hot pepper sauce
1	clove garlic, minced
2	pounds boneless pork country-style ribs
	Hot cooked noodles

For sauce, in a 3½- or 4-quart crockery cooker combine undrained tomatoes, celery, sweet pepper, onion, tapioca, sugar, dried basil (if using), salt, black pepper, hot pepper sauce, and garlic. Add ribs; stir to coat ribs with sauce.

Cover; cook on low-heat setting for 8 to 10 hours or on high-heat setting for 4 to 5 hours.

Transfer meat to a serving platter. Skim fat from sauce. Stir in fresh basil (if using). Spoon some of the sauce over meat. Serve with hot cooked noodles. Pass remaining sauce. Makes 6 servings.

Nutrition facts per serving: 314 calories, 21 g protein, 12 g carbohydrate, 20 g total fat (8 g saturated), 79 mg cholesterol, 477 mg sodium

cheesy scalloped potatoes and ham

Frozen hash brown potatoes and cheese soup simplify this old-fashioned favorite.

1   24-ounce package loose-pack frozen hash brown potatoes with onion and sweet peppers

2   cups diced cooked ham (10 ounces)

1   2-ounce jar diced pimiento, drained

1   tablespoon snipped fresh parsley

1/4   teaspoon black pepper

1   11-ounce can condensed cheddar cheese soup

3/4   cup milk

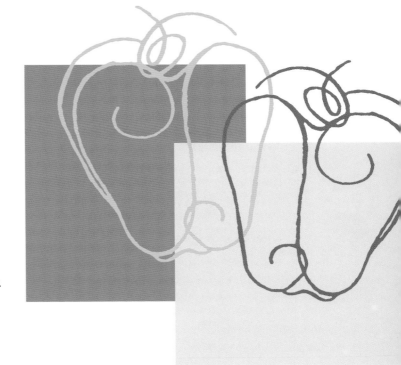

In a 3½-, 4-, or 5-quart crockery cooker combine frozen hash brown potatoes, ham, pimiento, parsley, and pepper.

In a medium bowl combine the soup and milk; pour over the potato mixture in the crockery cooker.

Cover; cook on low-heat setting for 7 to 9 hours or on high-heat setting for 3½ to 4 hours. Stir before serving. Makes 4 servings.

Nutrition facts per serving: 470 calories, 24 g protein, 42 g carbohydrate, 24 g total fat (11 g saturated), 43 mg cholesterol, 1,454 mg sodium

fruit-stuffed ham loaf

Use a quick-read thermometer to make sure the ham loaf is thoroughly cooked. The thermometer should register 170°.

¾ cup mixed dried fruit bits

2 tablespoons apple butter

1 beaten egg

¼ cup milk

½ cup graham cracker crumbs

¼ teaspoon pepper

1 pound ground cooked ham

½ pound ground pork

½ cup packed brown sugar

2 tablespoons apple juice

½ teaspoon dry mustard

In a small bowl combine fruit bits and apple butter. In a medium bowl combine egg, milk, graham cracker crumbs, and pepper. Add ground ham and pork to egg mixture; mix well.

Crisscross three 18×2-inch foil strips (place on a sheet of waxed paper to keep counter clean). In center of the foil strips pat half of the meat mixture into a 6-inch circle.

Spread fruit mixture on meat circle to within ½ inch of edges. On another sheet of waxed paper pat remaining meat mixture into a 6½-inch circle; invert on top of the first circle. Remove paper. Press edges of meat to seal well. Bringing up foil strips, lift and transfer meat and foil to a 3½-, 4-, or 5- quart crockery cooker. Press meat away from sides of the cooker to avoid burning.

Cover; cook on low-heat setting for 6 to 7 hours or on high-heat setting for 3 to 3½ hours.

In a small bowl combine brown sugar, apple juice, and dry mustard. Spread over meat. Cover; cook on low-heat setting or high-heat setting for 30 minutes.

Using foil strips, carefully lift ham loaf and transfer to a serving plate; discard the foil strips. Serve ham loaf with glaze. Makes 6 servings.

Nutrition facts per serving: 336 calories, 22 g protein, 40 g carbohydrate, 10 g total fat (2 g saturated), 91 mg cholesterol, 1,049 mg sodium

spaghetti sauce italiano

Start this spicy blended sauce in the morning—then forget about it until dinner!

½ pound bulk Italian sausage

¼ pound ground beef

½ cup chopped onion

1 clove garlic, minced

1 14½-ounce can tomatoes, cut up

1 8-ounce can tomato sauce

1 4-ounce can sliced mushrooms, drained

½ cup chopped green sweet pepper

2 tablespoons quick-cooking tapioca

1 bay leaf

1 teaspoon dried Italian seasoning, crushed

⅛ teaspoon black pepper

Dash salt

Hot cooked spaghetti

In a skillet cook sausage, ground beef, onion, and garlic until meat is brown. Drain off fat.

Meanwhile, in a 3½- or 4-quart crockery cooker combine undrained tomatoes, tomato sauce, mushrooms, sweet pepper, tapioca, bay leaf, Italian seasoning, black pepper, and salt. Stir in meat mixture.

Cover; cook on low-heat setting for 8 to 10 hours or on high-heat setting for 4 to 5 hours. Discard bay leaf. Serve over hot cooked spaghetti. Makes 4 or 5 servings.

Nutrition facts per serving: 491 calories, 24 g protein, 64 g carbohydrate, 16 g total fat (5 g saturated), 50 mg cholesterol, 1,107 mg sodium

tips from the kitchen

fix it and freeze ahead With a large capacity crockery cooker, you can cook once and have enough leftovers for two or three more dinners. To freeze leftovers, cool the hot food by placing it in a bowl set over another bowl filled with ice water. Transfer the cooled food to freezer-safe containers. Label and freeze (see tip, page 54).

To reheat, do not use your crockery cooker. Place the frozen food in an appropriate-sized saucepan; cook and stir over low heat until boiling. (Or, place food in an oven-safe casserole dish and bake in a 400° oven for 1 to 2 hours, stirring once during baking.)

lemon-mustard-sauced lamb dinner

Potatoes, carrots, and artichoke hearts complement the savory lamb in this hearty one-dish meal.

1	2- to 2½-pound boneless lamb shoulder roast
½	teaspoon lemon-pepper seasoning
½	teaspoon dry mustard
1	tablespoon cooking oil
4	medium potatoes, quartered
1½	cups packaged peeled baby carrots
1	cup chicken broth
3	tablespoons Dijon-style mustard
2	tablespoons quick-cooking tapioca
1	tablespoon lemon juice
½	teaspoon dried rosemary, crushed
¼	teaspoon finely shredded lemon peel
¼	teaspoon black pepper
2	cloves garlic, minced
1	9-ounce package frozen artichoke hearts, thawed

Trim fat from lamb roast. If necessary, cut roast to fit into a 3½- or 4-quart crockery cooker. In a small bowl combine lemon-pepper seasoning and dry mustard. Sprinkle evenly over sides of lamb roast; rub lightly with fingers. In a large skillet brown the roast slowly on all sides in hot oil.

Meanwhile, place potatoes and carrots in a 3½- or 4-quart crockery cooker. Place meat on top of vegetables. For sauce, in a small bowl combine broth, Dijon-style mustard, tapioca, lemon juice, rosemary, lemon peel, black pepper, and garlic; pour over all in crockery cooker.

Cover; cook on low-heat setting for 10 to 12 hours or on high-heat setting for 4 to 5 hours.

If using low-heat setting, turn to high-heat setting. Add thawed artichoke hearts. Cover and cook on high-heat setting 30 minutes. Skim fat from sauce and serve sauce with roast. Makes 4 servings.

Nutrition facts per serving: 590 calories, 47 g protein, 52 g carbohydrate, 21 g total fat (7 g saturated), 133 mg cholesterol, 824 mg sodium

sloppy joes

Prepare this classic with ground raw pork, chicken, or turkey if you're in the mood for a change. Use the leftovers as a topping for hot dogs.

1½   pounds ground beef

1   cup chopped onion

2   cloves garlic, minced

¾   cup catsup

½   cup chopped green sweet pepper

½   cup chopped celery

¼   cup water

1   to 2 tablespoons brown sugar

2   tablespoons prepared mustard

2   tablespoons vinegar

2   tablespoons Worcestershire sauce

1½   teaspoons chili powder

8   hamburger buns, split and toasted

In a large skillet cook ground beef, onion, and garlic until meat is brown. Drain off fat.

Meanwhile, in a 3½- or 4-quart crockery cooker combine catsup, sweet pepper, celery, water, brown sugar, mustard, vinegar, Worcestershire sauce, and chili powder. Stir in meat mixture.

Cover; cook on low-heat setting for 6 to 8 hours or on high-heat setting for 3 to 4 hours. Spoon into toasted buns. Makes 8 servings.

Nutrition facts per serving: 340 calories, 21 g protein, 35 g carbohydrate, 13 g total fat (5 g saturated), 53 mg cholesterol, 690 mg sodium

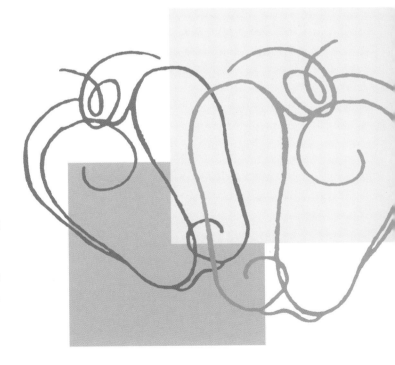

beef and peppers sandwiches

With these sandwiches, you can incorporate your crockery cooker into an informal buffet. Add a tray of fresh vegetables and dip and a pitcher of iced tea to the menu.

1   2½- to 3-pound boneless beef chuck
    pot roast, cut into 1-inch cubes

1   large onion, chopped

¼   cup Worcestershire sauce

1   tablespoon instant beef bouillon granules

1   teaspoon dried oregano, crushed

½   teaspoon dried basil, crushed

½   teaspoon dried thyme, crushed

2   cloves garlic, minced

½   cup chopped pepperoncini (Italian pickled
    peppers) or other pickled peppers

8   hoagie buns or kaiser rolls,
    split and toasted

6   ounces sliced Swiss cheese

In a 3½- or 4-quart crockery cooker combine meat, onion, Worcestershire sauce, bouillon granules, oregano, basil, thyme, and garlic.

Cover; cook on low-heat setting for 10 hours or on high-heat setting for 5 to 6 hours. Stir to break up meat cubes. Stir in chopped pepperoncini. Cook, uncovered, on high-heat setting for 30 minutes, stirring often to break up meat.

Using a slotted spoon, place meat mixture on the bun bottoms. Top each sandwich with cheese. Broil sandwiches 4 inches from heat about 1 minute or until cheese melts. Add bun tops. Makes 8 servings.

Nutrition facts per serving: 493 calories, 46 g protein, 35 g carbohydrate, 18 g total fat (8 g saturated), 122 mg cholesterol, 1,009 mg sodium

tips from the kitchen

frozen food timeline
Once a food is frozen, it will not keep forever. Label frozen items with a date so you can enjoy them at their best. Freeze soups, stews, and meat dishes with gravy for up to 3 months. Meat with vegetables and/or pasta can be frozen for up to 1 month.

To prevent freezer burn, store food in freezer containers with tightly fitting lids or wrap food tightly in freezer packaging material.

barbecued beef sandwiches

Since beef brisket needs long, slow cooking to become tender, we recommend that you use the low-heat setting on your crockery cooker for this recipe.

1 2¹/₂- to 3-pound fresh beef brisket

1 10-ounce can chopped tomatoes with green chile peppers

1 8-ounce can applesauce

¹/₂ of a 6-ounce can (¹/₃ cup) tomato paste

¹/₄ cup soy sauce

¹/₄ cup packed brown sugar

1 tablespoon Worcestershire sauce

10 to 12 hamburger buns, split and toasted

Trim fat from meat. If necessary, cut meat to fit into a 3½-, 4-, or 5-quart crockery cooker; reserve trimmings for another use. Place meat in cooker. In a medium bowl stir together the undrained tomatoes, applesauce, tomato paste, soy sauce, brown sugar, and Worcestershire sauce; pour over meat.

Cover; cook on low-heat setting about 10 hours or until meat is tender. Remove meat, reserving juices; cover to keep warm.

Pour cooking juices into a large saucepan. Bring to boiling; reduce heat. Boil gently, uncovered, for 15 to 20 minutes or until reduced to desired consistency, stirring frequently. Thinly slice meat across the grain. Place meat on bun bottoms. Drizzle with cooking juices; add bun tops. Makes 10 to 12 servings.

Nutrition facts per serving: 309 calories, 27 g protein, 23 g carbohydrate, 12 g total fat (4 g saturated), 78 mg cholesterol, 661 mg sodium

savory poultry simmers

Plum-Sauced Chicken in Tortillas
(see recipe, page 58)

plum-sauced chicken in tortillas

Hoisin sauce, a reddish-brown sauce with a sweet-and-spicy flavor, can be found in the Asian section of the supermarket. (Recipe pictured on pages 56–57).

  1   16-ounce can whole, unpitted purple
      plums, drained

  1   cup hot-style vegetable juice

 ¼   cup hoisin sauce

4½   teaspoons quick-cooking tapioca

  2   teaspoons grated fresh ginger

 ½   teaspoon five-spice powder

  1   pound skinless, boneless chicken thighs

  6   7- to 8-inch flour tortillas, warmed*

  2   cups packaged shredded broccoli (broccoli
      slaw mix) or packaged shredded cabbage
      with carrot (coleslaw mix)

Remove pits from plums. Place plums in a blender container or food processor bowl. Cover and blend or process until smooth. Transfer plums to a 3½- or 4-quart crockery cooker. Stir in vegetable juice, hoisin sauce, tapioca, fresh ginger, and five-spice powder. Rinse chicken; pat dry. Cut chicken into strips. Stir chicken strips into mixture in crockery cooker.

Cover; cook on low-heat setting for 4 to 5 hours or on high-heat setting for 2 to 2½ hours. Remove chicken from cooker, reserving juices.

Spoon about ⅓ cup chicken mixture onto each warm tortilla just below the center. Drizzle with the reserved juices. Top each with ⅓ cup shredded slaw mix. Roll up tortilla. Makes 6 servings.

*Note: To warm tortillas, wrap in foil and heat in a 350° oven for 5 minutes.

Nutrition facts per serving: 271 calories, 13 g protein, 38 g carbohydrate, 6 g total fat (2 g saturated), 36 mg cholesterol, 539 mg sodium

tips from the kitchen

storing leftovers For safety reasons, after cooking, food should not be left in your crockery cooker to cool. Also, don't use the cooker as a storage container or place it in the refrigerator.

To store cooked food properly, remove any remaining food from your cooker. (If the food is still very hot, transfer it to a large, shallow container to cool.) After it has cooled sufficiently (hold it no longer than 2 hours at room temperature), transfer the food to storage containers made specifically for the refrigerator or freezer. Cover tightly; label and date containers. Store in the refrigerator or freezer.

old world chicken

Juniper berries, native to Europe and America, add an intriguing flavor to this dish. Look for juniper berries in the spice section of large supermarkets or at specialty food stores.

2	slices bacon
2¹/₂	to 3 pounds meaty chicken pieces (breasts, thighs, and drumsticks), skinned
1	teaspoon whole juniper berries
3	medium carrots, cut into ¹/₂-inch pieces
¹/₄	cup chopped shallots or onion
¹/₄	cup coarsely chopped celery
¹/₂	cup chicken broth
¹/₄	cup dry red wine or port
2	tablespoons quick-cooking tapioca
1¹/₂	teaspoons snipped fresh thyme or ¹/₂ teaspoon dried thyme, crushed
1	teaspoon snipped fresh rosemary or ¹/₄ teaspoon dried rosemary, crushed
¹/₄	teaspoon salt
¹/₈	teaspoon pepper
1	cup frozen peas
2	tablespoons currant jelly
	Hot cooked rice

In a small skillet cook bacon until crisp; drain on paper towels. Crumble bacon; set aside. Rinse chicken; pat dry and set aside. For spice bag, cut a double thickness of 100 percent cotton cheesecloth into a 6-inch square. Place juniper berries in center of cheesecloth square. Bring corners of cheesecloth together and tie with clean cotton string.

Place carrots, shallots or onion, celery, and spice bag in a 3½-, 4-, or 5-quart crockery cooker. Add chicken. Sprinkle with bacon. In a small bowl combine broth, wine or port, tapioca, dried thyme and rosemary (if using), salt, and pepper; pour over all.

Cover; cook on low-heat setting for 6 to 7 hours or on high-heat setting for 3 to 3½ hours or until chicken is tender. Using a slotted spoon, transfer chicken and carrots to a serving platter; keep warm. If using low-heat setting, turn to high-heat setting. Stir in the peas and the fresh thyme and rosemary (if using). Cook on high-heat setting for 5 minutes. Remove spice bag. Skim off fat. Add currant jelly to mixture in crockery cooker; stir until smooth. Pour over chicken mixture. Serve with hot cooked rice. Makes 4 servings.

Nutrition facts per serving: 474 calories, 43 g protein, 45 g carbohydrate, 11 g total fat (3 g saturated), 118 mg cholesterol, 500 mg sodium

chicken and sausage paella

The flavor of paella comes from saffron, the dried threads or stigmas of the purple crocus. Saffron lends a yellow color, bittersweet flavor, and wonderful aroma.

2½ to 3 pounds meaty chicken pieces (breasts, thighs, and drumsticks)

1 tablespoon cooking oil

8 ounces cooked smoked turkey sausage, halved lengthwise and sliced

1 large onion, sliced

3 cloves garlic, minced

2 tablespoons snipped fresh thyme or 2 teaspoons dried thyme, crushed

¼ teaspoon black pepper

⅛ teaspoon thread saffron or ¼ teaspoon ground turmeric

1 14½-ounce can reduced-sodium chicken broth (1¾ cups)

½ cup water

2 cups chopped tomatoes

2 yellow or green sweet peppers, cut into very thin bite-size strips

1 cup frozen green peas

Hot cooked rice

Skin chicken. Rinse chicken; pat dry. In a large skillet brown chicken pieces, half at a time, in hot oil. Drain off fat. Place chicken pieces, turkey sausage, and onion in a 3½-, 4-, or 5-quart crockery cooker. Sprinkle with garlic, dried thyme (if using), black pepper, and saffron or turmeric. Pour broth and water over all.

Cover; cook on low-heat setting for 7 to 8 hours or on high-heat setting for 3½ to 4 hours. Add the tomatoes, sweet peppers, peas, and the fresh thyme (if using). Cover; let stand for 5 minutes. Serve over the hot cooked rice. Makes 6 servings.

Nutrition facts per serving: 397 calories, 36 g protein, 35 g carbohydrate, 12 g total fat (3 g saturated), 101 mg cholesterol, 608 mg sodium

chicken curry

This bold flavored chicken and vegetable dish is a must-try for Indian food lovers!

12 ounces skinless, boneless chicken breast halves or thighs

4 medium potatoes, cut into 1-inch chunks

1 medium green sweet pepper, cut into 1-inch pieces

1 medium onion, sliced

1 cup chopped tomato

1 tablespoon ground coriander

2 teaspoons grated fresh ginger or 1/2 teaspoon ground ginger

1 1/2 teaspoons paprika

3/4 teaspoon salt

1/2 to 1 teaspoon crushed red pepper

1/2 teaspoon ground turmeric

1/4 teaspoon ground cinnamon

1/8 teaspoon ground cloves

3/4 cup chicken broth

1 tablespoon cornstarch

1 tablespoon cold water

Rinse chicken; pat dry. Cut chicken into 1-inch pieces.

Place potatoes, sweet pepper, and onion in 3½- or 4-quart crockery cooker. Place chicken on top of vegetables.

For sauce, in a medium bowl combine tomato, coriander, fresh ginger, paprika, salt, red pepper, turmeric, cinnamon, and cloves; stir in chicken broth. Pour sauce over chicken pieces.

Cover; cook on low-heat setting for 8 to 10 hours or on high-setting setting for 4 to 5 hours.

If using low-heat setting, turn to high-heat setting. Stir cornstarch into cold water; stir into broth. Cover and cook on high-heat setting 10 to 15 minutes or until thickened and bubbly. Makes 4 servings.

Nutrition facts per serving: 288 calories, 22 g protein, 43 g carbohydrate, 3 g total fat (1 g saturated), 45 mg cholesterol, 607 mg sodium

herbed chicken and vegetables

Chicken, potatoes, carrots, celery, and onion simmered in a delicate, wine-flavored sauce make an irresistible one-dish meal.

3 pounds chicken drumsticks or thighs, skinned

2 tablespoons cooking oil

1 cup chicken broth

1/2 cup dry white wine

1 tablespoon snipped fresh parsley

1/2 teaspoon salt

1/2 teaspoon dried rosemary, crushed

1/2 teaspoon dried thyme, crushed

1/4 teaspoon pepper

1 clove garlic, minced

4 medium potatoes, quartered

4 medium carrots, cut into 1/2-inch pieces

2 stalks celery, cut into 1-inch pieces

1 small onion, sliced

2 tablespoons cornstarch

2 tablespoons cold water

Rinse chicken; pat dry. In a skillet brown chicken pieces, half at a time, in hot oil.

In a medium bowl combine the chicken broth, wine, parsley, salt, rosemary, thyme, pepper, and garlic.

Place potatoes, carrots, celery, and onion in a 3½-, 4-, or 5-quart crockery cooker. Place chicken pieces on top of vegetables. Pour broth mixture over chicken.

Cover; cook on low-heat setting for 8 to 9 hours or on high-heat setting for 4 to 4½ hours.

Using a slotted spoon, remove chicken and vegetables to a platter; keep warm.

For gravy, skim fat from cooking juices. Strain juices into saucepan. Stir cornstarch into cold water; stir into juices in saucepan. Cook and stir until thickened and bubbly. Cook and stir 2 minutes more. Pass the gravy with the chicken and vegetables. Makes 6 servings.

Nutrition facts per serving: 338 calories, 27 g protein, 31 g carbohydrate, 10 g total fat (2 g saturated), 79 mg cholesterol, 416 mg sodium

easy italian chicken breasts

Try a variation on this recipe! Substitute boneless, skinless chicken thighs for the breasts, or use spinach or red sweet pepper fettuccine. Regular frozen green beans work well, too.

12 ounces skinless, boneless chicken breast halves

1 9-ounce package frozen Italian-style green beans

1 cup fresh mushrooms, quartered

1 small onion, sliced ¼ inch thick

1 14½-ounce can Italian-style stewed tomatoes

1 6-ounce can Italian-style tomato paste

1 teaspoon dried Italian seasoning, crushed

2 cloves garlic, minced

Hot cooked fettuccine

Grated Parmesan cheese (optional)

Rinse chicken; pat dry. Cut chicken into 1-inch pieces.

Place green beans, mushrooms, and onion in a 3½- or 4-quart crockery cooker. Place chicken on top of the vegetables.

In a small bowl combine undrained tomatoes, tomato paste, Italian seasoning, and garlic. Pour over chicken.

Cover; cook on low-heat setting for 5 to 6 hours or on high-heat setting for 2½ to 3 hours. Serve over hot cooked fettuccine. If desired, pass grated Parmesan cheese. Makes 4 servings.

Nutrition facts per serving: 308 calories, 24 g protein, 44 g carbohydrate, 4 g total fat (1 g saturated), 45 mg cholesterol, 799 mg sodium

plum-spiced chicken and vegetables

With the look and taste of a stir-fry, this easy-to-prepare dish is even better—it doesn't take a lot of last-minute preparation!

2 to 2½ pounds chicken breasts, thighs, and/or legs, skinned

2 cups bias-sliced carrots

2 tablespoons quick-cooking tapioca

1 8-ounce can tomato sauce

½ cup plum jam or preserves

2 tablespoons vinegar

½ teaspoon ground ginger

½ teaspoon ground cinnamon

1 6-ounce package frozen pea pods, thawed

Hot cooked rice

¼ cup bias-sliced green onions

Rinse chicken; pat dry. Set chicken aside.

Place carrots in a 3½- or 4-quart crockery cooker; sprinkle with tapioca. Place chicken pieces on top of carrots.

In a medium bowl combine tomato sauce, plum jam or preserves, vinegar, ginger, and cinnamon. Pour over chicken.

Cover; cook on low-heat setting for 7 to 8 hours or on high-heat setting for 3½ to 4 hours. Stir in thawed pea pods. Arrange chicken over rice on platter. Skim fat from sauce; pour over chicken. Sprinkle with sliced green onions. Makes 6 servings.

Nutrition facts per serving: 361 calories, 24 g protein, 54 g carbohydrate, 5 g total fat (1 g saturated), 61 mg cholesterol, 319 mg sodium

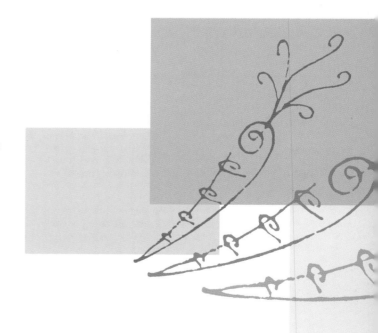

orange teriyaki chicken

If your family includes white meat lovers and dark meat lovers, use a combination of chicken breasts and thighs. Both are equally delicious with this sauce that's sweet and full of flavor.

1 pound skinless, boneless chicken breast halves or thighs

1 16-ounce package loose-pack frozen broccoli, baby carrots, and water chestnuts

2 tablespoons quick-cooking tapioca

1/2 cup chicken broth

2 tablespoons brown sugar

2 tablespoons teriyaki sauce

1 teaspoon dry mustard

1 teaspoon finely shredded orange peel

1/2 teaspoon ground ginger

Hot cooked rice

Rinse chicken; pat dry. Cut chicken into 1-inch pieces.

Place frozen vegetables in a 3½-, 4-, or 5-quart crockery cooker. Sprinkle tapioca over vegetables. Place chicken pieces on top of vegetables.

For sauce, in a small bowl combine chicken broth, brown sugar, teriyaki sauce, mustard, orange peel, and ginger. Pour sauce over chicken pieces.

Cover; cook on low-heat setting for 4 to 6 hours or on high-heat setting for 2 to 3 hours. Serve with hot cooked rice. Makes 4 servings.

Nutrition facts per serving: 303 calories, 27 g protein, 39 g carbohydrate, 4 g total fat (1 g saturated), 60 mg cholesterol, 543 mg sodium

spicy ginger and tomato chicken

A superb sauce of tomato, ginger, garlic, and crushed red pepper complements this chicken.

1   2½- to 3-pound cut up broiler-fryer chicken, skinned

2   14½-ounce cans tomatoes

2   tablespoons quick-cooking tapioca

1   tablespoon grated fresh ginger

1   tablespoon snipped fresh cilantro or parsley

4   cloves garlic, minced

2   teaspoons brown sugar

½   to 1 teaspoon crushed red pepper

½   teaspoon salt

    Hot cooked couscous or rice

Rinse chicken; pat dry. Place chicken pieces in a 3½- or 4-quart crockery cooker.

Drain 1 can of tomatoes; chop tomatoes from both cans. For sauce, in a medium bowl combine both cans of tomatoes, tapioca, fresh ginger, cilantro or parsley, garlic, brown sugar, crushed red pepper, and salt. Pour sauce over chicken.

Cover; cook on low-heat setting for 6 to 7 hours or on high-heat setting for 3 to 3½ hours. Skim fat from sauce. Serve sauce with chicken and couscous or rice. Makes 6 servings.

Nutrition facts per serving: 332 calories, 25 g protein, 33 g carbohydrate, 11 g total fat (3 g saturated), 66 mg cholesterol, 507 mg sodium

southwestern barbecue-style chicken

Serve this south-of-the-border chicken with black beans, avocado slices, and warmed flour tortillas.

2 to 2½ pounds chicken breasts, thighs, and/or legs, skinned

½ cup tomato sauce

2 tablespoons jalapeño pepper jelly

2 tablespoons lime or lemon juice

2 tablespoons quick-cooking tapioca

1 teaspoon brown sugar

1 teaspoon ground cumin

¼ to ½ teaspoon crushed red pepper

Rinse chicken; pat dry. Set chicken aside.

In a 3½- or 4-quart crockery cooker combine tomato sauce, jelly, lime or lemon juice, tapioca, brown sugar, cumin, and red pepper. Place chicken pieces, meaty sides down, on top of sauce mixture.

Cover; cook on low-heat setting for 6 to 7 hours or on high-heat setting for 3 to 3½ hours. Makes 4 to 6 servings.

Nutrition facts per serving: 227 calories, 26 g protein, 15 g carbohydrate, 7 g total fat (2 g saturated), 81 mg cholesterol, 264 mg sodium

italian-herbed chicken

Tender chicken pieces with chunks of vegetables produce a Mediterranean-flavored meal perfect over pasta.

2 to 2¹/₂ pounds chicken breasts, thighs, and/or legs, skinned

2 cups sliced fresh mushrooms

1 14¹/₂-ounce can tomato wedges, drained

1 9-ounce package frozen artichoke hearts

¹/₂ cup sliced pitted ripe olives

3 tablespoons quick-cooking tapioca

³/₄ cup chicken broth

¹/₄ cup dry white wine or chicken broth

1 tablespoon dried Italian seasoning, crushed

Hot cooked linguine

Rinse chicken; pat dry. Set chicken aside.

In a 3¹/₂- or 4-quart crockery cooker combine the mushrooms, tomato wedges, frozen artichoke hearts, and olives. Sprinkle with tapioca. Place the chicken pieces on top of vegetables.

In a small bowl combine the chicken broth, white wine or broth, and Italian seasoning. Pour over the chicken.

Cover; cook on low-heat setting for 7 to 8 hours or on high-heat setting for 3¹/₂ to 4 hours. Serve with hot cooked linguine. Makes 4 to 6 servings.

Nutrition facts per serving: 397 calories, 35 g protein, 42 g carbohydrate, 10 g total fat (2 g saturated), 81 mg cholesterol, 538 mg sodium

tips from the kitchen

broth options When a recipe calls for chicken broth, beef broth, or vegetable broth, you can either make your own from scratch or use purchased products.

Canned chicken, beef, and vegetable broth are ready to use straight from the can. Instant bouillon granules and cubes can be purchased in beef, chicken, vegetable, and onion flavors. One cube or 1 teaspoon of granules mixed with 1 cup water makes an easy broth. (If you are watching your sodium intake, try lower sodium broth or bouillon and adjust the recipe's seasonings to taste.)

chicken with vegetables and stuffing

This casserole-style dinner tastes just like traditional chicken with stuffing—but it's quicker and easier to prepare. It's a great use for leftover chicken or turkey.

1   6-ounce package chicken flavor stuffing mix

2½   cups chopped cooked chicken

2   cups zucchini, cut into ½-inch pieces

2   cups sliced fresh mushrooms

1   medium red or green sweet pepper, cut into ½-inch pieces

½   cup chopped onion

1   10¾-ounce can condensed cream of chicken soup or cream of mushroom soup

Prepare stuffing mix according to package directions, except reduce water to ½ cup. (Stuffing will not be completely moistened.) Set aside.

In a large bowl combine chicken, zucchini, mushrooms, sweet pepper, and onion. Stir in soup.

Place half of the chicken-vegetable mixture in a 3½-, 4-, or 5-quart crockery cooker; top with half of the stuffing. Repeat layers.

Cover; cook on low-heat setting for 5 to 6 hours or on high-heat setting for 2½ to 3 hours. Makes 6 servings.

Nutrition facts per serving: 315 calories, 24 g protein, 29 g carbohydrate, 11 g total fat (3 g saturated), 52 mg cholesterol, 976 mg sodium

sweet 'n' spicy turkey

Now that you can buy turkey parts, rather than the whole bird, it's economical to use turkey in your favorite dishes. Here just two thighs serve six people.

2	turkey thighs (2½ to 2¾ pounds total), skinned
²/₃	cup chopped onion
¾	cup cranberry juice cocktail
¼	cup Dijon-style mustard
¼	teaspoon ground red pepper
½	cup dried cranberries or cherries
2	teaspoons cornstarch
1	tablespoon cold water
3	cups hot cooked barley
1	medium nectarine or pear, cored and chopped

Rinse turkey thighs; pat dry. Place turkey thighs in the bottom of a 3½- or 4-quart crockery cooker. Add onion. In a small bowl combine cranberry juice cocktail, mustard, and red pepper; pour over all.

Cover; cook on low-heat setting for 5 to 6 hours or on high-heat setting for 2½ to 3 hours. Remove turkey; keep warm.

For sauce, strain cooking juices. Measure 1½ cups juices (if necessary, add water to make 1½ cups). In a small saucepan combine juices and cranberries or cherries. Stir cornstarch into cold water; add to mixture in saucepan. Cook and stir over medium heat until thickened and bubbly. Cook and stir for 2 minutes more. To serve, toss hot cooked barley with nectarine or pear. Serve turkey and sauce over barley mixture. Makes 6 servings.

Nutrition facts per serving: 436 calories, 42 g protein, 41 g carbohydrate, 11 g total fat (3 g saturated), 116 mg cholesterol, 365 mg sodium

turkey meatballs and gravy

No one will believe this rich tasting gravy starts with a mix.

2 beaten eggs

³/₄ cup fine dry seasoned bread crumbs

¹/₂ cup finely chopped onion

¹/₂ cup finely chopped celery

2 tablespoons snipped fresh parsley

¹/₄ teaspoon pepper

¹/₈ teaspoon garlic powder

2 pounds ground raw turkey

1¹/₂ teaspoons cooking oil

1 10³/₄-ounce can reduced-sodium condensed cream of mushroom soup

1 cup water

1 ¹⁵/₁₆-ounce envelope turkey gravy mix

¹/₂ teaspoon finely shredded lemon peel

¹/₂ teaspoon dried thyme, crushed

1 bay leaf

Hot mashed potatoes or buttered cooked noodles

Snipped fresh parsley (optional)

In a large bowl combine eggs, bread crumbs, onion, celery, 2 tablespoons parsley, pepper, and garlic powder. Add ground turkey and mix well. Shape into 1½-inch balls.

In a large skillet brown meatballs, half at a time, in hot oil. If necessary, add additional oil. Drain meatballs. Transfer to a 3½- or 4-quart crockery cooker.

In a medium bowl combine soup, water, gravy mix, lemon peel, thyme, and bay leaf. Pour over meatballs.

Cover; cook on low-heat setting for 6 to 8 hours or on high-heat setting for 3 to 4 hours. Discard bay leaf. Serve with mashed potatoes or noodles. If desired, sprinkle with additional snipped fresh parsley. Makes 8 servings.

Nutrition facts per serving: 314 calories, 21 g protein, 25 g carbohydrate, 14 g total fat (3 g saturated), 98 mg cholesterol, 916 mg sodium

Raspberry Fudgey Brownies
(see recipe, page 82)

simple sides
& sweets

new england crock-style baked beans

No need to heat up your kitchen by turning the oven on—the crockery cooker slow "bakes" beans perfectly.

1 pound dry navy beans or dry Great Northern beans (2⅓ cups)

8 cups cold water

1 cup chopped onion

¼ pound salt pork, chopped, or 6 slices bacon, cooked, drained, and crumbled

1 cup water

½ cup molasses

⅓ cup packed brown sugar

1 teaspoon dry mustard

¼ teaspoon pepper

Rinse beans; drain. In a large saucepan or kettle combine beans and the 8 cups water. Bring to boiling; reduce heat. Simmer, covered, for 1½ to 2 hours or until beans are tender.

Drain beans. In a 3½- or 4-quart crockery cooker combine drained beans, onion, and salt pork or bacon. Add 1 cup water, molasses, brown sugar, dry mustard, and pepper. Stir to combine.

Cover; cook on low-heat setting for 10 to 12 hours or on high-heat setting for 5 to 6 hours. Stir before serving. Makes 12 servings.

Nutrition facts per serving: 257 calories, 8 g protein, 39 g carbohydrate, 8 g total fat (3 g saturated), 8 mg cholesterol, 145 mg sodium

baked bean quintet

Next time you need a side dish for a backyard barbecue, remember this intriguing twist on baked beans. It makes enough for a crowd.

1 large onion, chopped

6 slices bacon, cut up

1 clove garlic, minced

1 16-ounce can lima beans, drained and rinsed

1 16-ounce can pork and beans in tomato sauce

1 15½-ounce can red kidney beans, drained and rinsed

1 15-ounce can butter beans, drained and rinsed

1 15-ounce can garbanzo beans, drained and rinsed

³/₄ cup catsup

¹/₂ cup molasses

¹/₄ cup packed brown sugar

1 tablespoon prepared mustard

1 tablespoon Worcestershire sauce

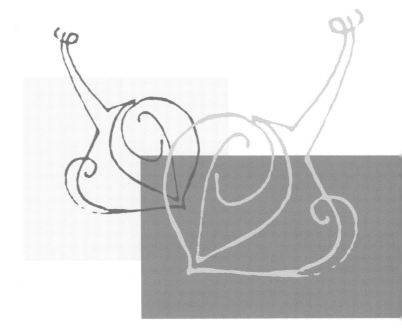

In a skillet cook onion, bacon, and garlic until bacon is done. Drain off fat. In large bowl combine onion mixture, all the beans, catsup, molasses, brown sugar, mustard, and Worcestershire sauce.

Transfer bean mixture to a 3½- or 4-quart crockery cooker. Cover; cook on low-heat setting for 10 to 12 hours or on high-heat setting for 4 to 5 hours. Makes 12 to 16 servings.

Nutrition facts per serving: 236 calories, 11 g protein, 46 g carbohydrate, 3 g total fat (1 g saturated), 5 mg cholesterol, 768 mg sodium

creamy ranch potatoes

So easy! Tote this 4-ingredient side dish to your next potluck meal.

2 pounds small red potatoes, quartered

1 8-ounce package cream cheese, softened

1 envelope buttermilk ranch dry salad dressing mix

1 10¾-ounce can condensed cream of potato soup

Place potatoes in a 3½-quart crockery cooker. In a small bowl combine cream cheese and salad dressing mix. Stir in soup. Pour over potatoes.

Cover; cook on low-heat setting for 7 to 9 hours or on high-heat setting for 3½ to 4½ hours. Stir to blend before serving. Makes 6 servings.

Nutrition facts per serving: 315 calories, 7 g protein, 40 g carbohydrate, 14 g total fat (9 g saturated), 45 mg cholesterol, 665 mg sodium

tips from the kitchen

start early If you plan to leave early in the morning, start your recipe preparations the previous night. If needed, precook the meat. Place cleaned and chopped vegetables, seasonings, and liquids into a bowl or the crockery liner if it is removable. Chill the meat and vegetables. The following morning, assemble all ingredients in the cooker, cover, and let the dish cook while you spend your time as you like.

hot german potato salad

This sweet and tangy, warm salad pairs well with roasted pork.

6 cups peeled potatoes, cut into
   ¹/₄-inch-thick slices (about 2 pounds)

1 cup chopped onion

1 cup chopped celery

1 cup water

²/₃ cup cider vinegar

¹/₄ cup sugar

2 tablespoons quick-cooking tapioca

1 teaspoon salt

³/₄ teaspoon celery seed

¹/₄ teaspoon pepper

6 slices bacon, crisp-cooked, drained,
   and crumbled

¹/₄ cup snipped fresh parsley

In a 3½- or 4-quart crockery cooker combine potatoes, onion, and celery.

In a medium bowl combine water, vinegar, sugar, tapioca, salt, celery seed, and pepper. Pour over potatoes.

Cover; cook on low-heat setting for 8 to 10 hours or on high-heat setting for 4 to 5 hours. Stir in bacon and parsley. Makes 8 servings.

Nutrition facts per serving: 162 calories, 4 g protein, 33 g carbohydrate, 3 g total fat (1 g saturated), 4 mg cholesterol, 371 mg sodium

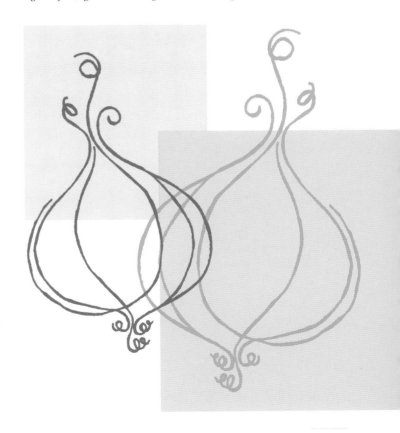

coconut-pecan sweet potatoes

Need more servings for a holiday meal? Double the ingredients and cook them in a 5- or 6-quart crockery cooker.

2	pounds sweet potatoes, peeled and shredded
1/3	cup packed brown sugar
1/4	cup margarine or butter, melted
1/4	cup coconut
1/4	cup broken pecans, toasted
1/4	teaspoon ground cinnamon
1/4	teaspoon coconut flavoring
1/4	teaspoon vanilla
	Toasted coconut (optional)

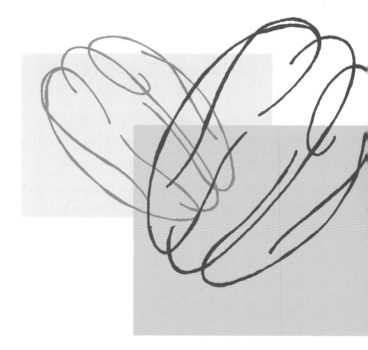

In a 3½-quart crockery cooker combine sweet potatoes, brown sugar, margarine or butter, coconut, pecans, and cinnamon.

Cover; cook on low-heat setting for 6 to 8 hours or on high-heat setting for 3 to 4 hours. Stir in coconut flavoring and vanilla. If desired, sprinkle with toasted coconut. Makes 4 to 6 servings.

Nutrition facts per serving: 408 calories, 4 g protein, 61 g carbohydrate, 18 g total fat (4 g saturated), 0 mg cholesterol, 157 mg sodium

crockery dressing

Cooking the stuffing in a crockery cooker frees up valuable space in the oven during busy holiday meal preparation.

12 cups dry bread cubes

2 cups sliced celery

1/2 cup finely chopped onion

1/4 cup snipped fresh parsley

1 1/2 teaspoons dried sage, crushed

1/2 teaspoon dried marjoram, crushed

1/4 teaspoon pepper

1 1/2 cups chicken broth

1/4 cup margarine or butter, melted

In a large bowl combine the dry bread cubes, celery, onion, parsley, sage, marjoram, and pepper.

Pour chicken broth and margarine or butter over bread mixture and toss gently. Place bread mixture in a 3½-, 4-, or 5-quart crockery cooker.

Cover; cook on low-heat setting for 4 to 5 hours. Makes 8 to 10 servings.

*Note: To prepare dry bread cubes, start with about 24 slices of bread. Cut the bread into ½-inch cubes and spread in a single layer in a large roasting pan. Bake in a 300° oven for 10 to 15 minutes or until dry; stir twice.

Nutrition facts per serving: 253 calories, 7 g protein, 37 g carbohydrate, 9 g total fat (2 g saturated), 0 mg cholesterol, 568 mg sodium

tips from the kitchen

recipe adaptations
Have a favorite recipe that you think would work well in a crockery cooker? To give it a try, follow these tips.

- Use recipes with less tender meat cuts that will benefit from long cooking times.

- Find a recipe in this book that is similar to yours to get a feel for appropriate quantities and liquid levels.

- Cut vegetables into pieces the size of those in your sample recipe; place them in the bottom of the cooker. Trim and brown the meat (if desired) and place on top of the vegetables.

- Reduce the liquid in your recipe by about half (except those dishes containing long grain rice).

- Cornstarch and flour break down during long cooking, so use quick-cooking tapioca for thickening (look for a tapioca-thickened recipe in this book). Or, thicken the juices in a saucepan at the end of cooking.

- Use the cooking times in the sample.

chocolate-peanut butter pudding cake

This pudding cake is a dessert lover's dream. A warm chocolate-peanut butter pudding develops under the cake layer as it "bakes." Spooned over ice cream, it is the best!

1	cup all-purpose flour
1/2	cup sugar
2	tablespoons unsweetened cocoa powder
1 1/2	teaspoons baking powder
1/2	cup milk
2	tablespoons cooking oil
1	teaspoon vanilla
3/4	cup peanut butter-flavored pieces
3/4	cup sugar
1/4	cup unsweetened cocoa powder
2	cups boiling water
1/2	cup chunky peanut butter
2	tablespoons chopped unsalted dry-roasted peanuts
	Vanilla ice cream (optional)

In a medium bowl stir together flour, the 1/2 cup sugar, the 2 tablespoons cocoa powder, and the baking powder. Add the milk, oil, and vanilla; stir until batter is smooth. Stir in the peanut butter pieces. Spread batter evenly in the bottom of a greased 3 1/2- or 4-quart crockery cooker.

In another medium bowl combine the 3/4 cup sugar and the 1/4 cup cocoa powder. Stir together boiling water and peanut butter; stir into the cocoa mixture. Pour evenly over the batter in the crockery cooker.

Cover; cook on high-heat setting for 2 to 2 1/2 hours or until a toothpick inserted 1 inch into the center of the cake comes out clean. Let stand, uncovered, for 30 to 40 minutes to cool slightly.

To serve, spoon pudding cake into dessert dishes. Sprinkle with chopped peanuts. If desired, serve with ice cream. Makes 8 servings.

Nutrition facts per serving: 417 calories, 10 g protein, 56 g carbohydrate, 18 g total fat (4 g saturated), 1 mg cholesterol, 196 mg sodium

cranberry bread pudding

Your crockery cooker is a perfect partner in creating spectacular desserts. This bread pudding steams unattended so you can return home to an out-of-this-world taste treat.

1 ½ cups half-and-half or light cream

½ of a 6-ounce package white baking bars or squares, coarsely chopped

⅓ cup snipped dried cranberries or dried cherries

2 beaten eggs

½ cup sugar

½ teaspoon ground ginger

3 cups dry ½-inch bread cubes (about 4½ slices)

¼ cup coarsely chopped pecans or hazelnuts

Whipped cream (optional)

Grated white baking bar (optional)

Ground ginger (optional)

In a small saucepan heat half-and-half or light cream over medium heat until very warm but not boiling. Remove from heat; add chopped white baking bar and cranberries or cherries. Stir until baking bar is melted.

In a large bowl combine eggs, sugar, and the ½ teaspoon ginger. Whisk in the cream mixture. Gently stir in bread cubes and nuts. Pour mixture into a 1-quart soufflé dish (dish will be full). Cover the dish tightly with foil.

Pour 1 cup warm water into a 3½-, 4-, or 5-quart crockery cooker. Tear off an 18×12-inch piece of heavy foil. Divide in half lengthwise. Fold each piece into thirds lengthwise. Crisscross the strips and place the soufflé dish in the center of the foil cross. Bringing up foil strips, lift the ends of the strips to transfer the dish and foil to the cooker. (Leave foil strips under dish.)

Cover; cook on low-heat setting for 4 hours or on high-heat setting for 2 hours. Using the foil strips, carefully lift dish out of cooker. Serve pudding warm or chilled. If desired, serve with whipped cream and sprinkle with grated white chocolate and additional ground ginger. Makes 6 servings.

Nutrition facts per serving: 360 calories, 7 g protein, 45 g carbohydrate, 17 g total fat (8 g saturated), 98 mg cholesterol, 177 mg sodium

raspberry fudgey brownies

Serve these fix-'em-and-forget-'em brownies plain or dressed up as brownie sundaes. Either way, they are scrumptious. (Recipe pictured on pages 72–73.)

½ cup margarine or butter

2 ounces unsweetened chocolate

2 eggs

¾ cup sugar

⅓ cup seedless red raspberry jam

1 teaspoon vanilla

¾ cup all-purpose flour

¼ teaspoon baking powder

Powdered sugar (optional)

Coffee or vanilla ice cream (optional)

Chocolate ice-cream topping (optional)

Fresh raspberries (optional)

Generously grease two 1-pint straight-sided, wide-mouthed canning jars. Flour the greased jars; set aside.

In a saucepan melt margarine or butter and chocolate over low heat. Remove from heat. Stir in eggs, sugar, jam, and vanilla. Using a spoon, beat lightly just until combined. Stir in flour and baking powder. Pour batter into prepared jars. Cover jars tightly with greased foil, greased side down. Place jars in a 3½- or 4-quart crockery cooker.* Pour 1 cup water around jars.

Cover; cook on high-heat setting for 3 to 3½ hours or until a toothpick inserted near the centers of brownie rolls comes out clean. Remove jars from cooker; cool for 10 minutes. Using a metal spatula, loosen brownies from sides of jars. Carefully remove rolls from jars. Place rolls on their sides on a wire rack; cool completely. To serve, cut each roll into 6 slices. If desired, sprinkle with powdered sugar and serve with ice cream, ice-cream topping, and/or fresh raspberries. Makes 12 brownie slices.

*Note: If both jars won't fit in your crockery cooker, cook 1 at a time; store second jar in refrigerator while first jar cooks.

Nutrition facts per brownie slice: 204 calories, 2 g protein, 26 g carbohydrate, 11 g total fat (0 g saturated), 36 mg cholesterol, 109 mg sodium

winter fruit compote

Spoon this spiced, warm autumn fruit combo atop cake slices or serve it in dessert bowls—plain or with vanilla ice cream.

3 medium cooking apples, cored and sliced

2 medium pears, cored and sliced

1 16-ounce can whole cranberry sauce

¼ cup water

½ teaspoon grated fresh ginger

½ teaspoon finely shredded lemon peel

½ teaspoon ground cinnamon

Toasted angel food cake slices
   or gingerbread (optional)

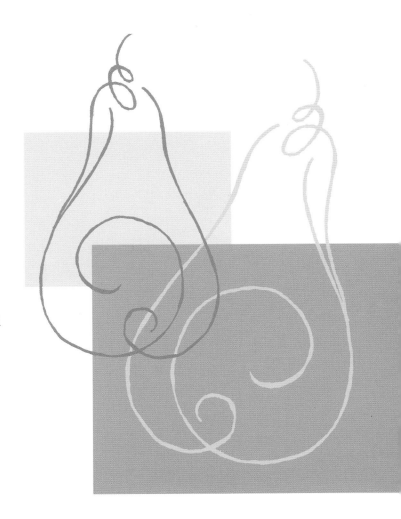

In a 3½- to 4-quart crockery cooker combine the apples, pears, cranberry sauce, water, ginger, lemon peel, and cinnamon. Cover and cook on the low-heat setting for 3 to 4 hours.

To serve, if desired, spoon warm fruit mixture over toasted angel food cake slices. (Or, serve in individual compote dishes.) Makes 8 to 10 servings.

Nutrition facts per serving: 135 calories, 0 g protein, 35 g carbohydrate, 0 g total fat, 0 mg cholesterol, 17 mg sodium

party snacks
& beverages

Clockwise from top left:

Tangy Cocktail Meatballs
(see recipe, page 88)

Buffalo Wings with Blue Cheese Dip
(see recipe, page 86)

Supreme Pizza Fondue
(see recipe, page 91)

buffalo wings with blue cheese dip

Need an appetizer for a houseful of guests? This sports bar favorite is great for an after-the-game party. Beer, celery sticks, and lots of napkins are all you need. (Recipe pictured on pages 84–85.)

16 chicken wings (about 3 pounds)

1½ cups bottled chili sauce

3 to 4 tablespoons bottled hot pepper sauce

1 recipe Blue Cheese Dip or bottled ranch salad dressing

Cut off and discard wing tips. Cut each wing at the joint to make 2 sections. Rinse chicken; pat dry.

Place chicken on the unheated rack of a broiler pan. Broil 4 to 5 inches from the heat about 10 minutes or until chicken is browned, turning once. Transfer chicken to a 3½- or 4-quart crockery cooker. Combine chili sauce and hot pepper sauce; pour over chicken wings.

Cover; cook on low-heat setting for 4 to 5 hours or on high-heat setting for 2 to 2½ hours. Serve chicken wings with Blue Cheese Dip or ranch salad dressing. Makes 32 appetizers.

Blue Cheese Dip: In a blender container combine one 8-ounce carton dairy sour cream; ½ cup mayonnaise or salad dressing; ½ cup crumbled blue cheese (2 ounces); 1 clove garlic, minced; and 1 tablespoon white wine vinegar or white vinegar. Cover and blend until smooth. Store dip, covered, in the refrigerator for up to 2 weeks. If desired, stir in 1 tablespoon thinly sliced green onion before serving.

Nutrition facts per appetizer with 1 tablespoon Blue Cheese Dip: 108 calories, 6 g protein, 3 g carbohydrate, 8 g total fat (3 g saturated), 21 mg cholesterol, 217 mg sodium

barbecue-style chicken wings

Vary the flavor of this party-starter by choosing your favorite style barbecue sauce.

16 chicken wings (about 3 pounds)

1½ cups bottled barbecue sauce

¼ cup honey

2 teaspoons prepared mustard

1½ teaspoons Worcestershire sauce

Cut off and discard wing tips. Cut each wing at the joint to make 2 sections. Rinse chicken; pat dry.

Place chicken on the unheated rack of a broiler pan. Broil 4 to 5 inches from the heat about 10 minutes or until chicken is browned, turning once. Transfer chicken to a 3½- or 4-quart crockery cooker.

For sauce, combine barbecue sauce, honey, mustard, and Worcestershire sauce; pour over chicken wings. Cover; cook on low-heat setting for 4 to 5 hours or on high-heat setting for 2 to 2½ hours. Makes 32 appetizers.

Nutrition facts per appetizer: 67 calories, 5 g protein, 4 g carbohydrate, 4 g total fat (1 g saturated), 14 mg cholesterol, 115 mg sodium

tips from the kitchen

party time with your cooker Looking for a way to give a party right after attending a game or some other away-from-home activity? That's easy with the help of the crockery cooker. Start with one or two of the recipes in this section (borrow another cooker if you want to make two recipes). Then, add purchased dips, chips, crackers, cheese, fresh fruit or vegetables, and a choice of beverages. Everyone, including you, will enjoy the food and fun.

tangy cocktail meatballs

If stuffing mix is unavailable, use croutons and lightly crush them with a rolling pin or the bottom of a mixing bowl. (Recipe pictured on page 84.)

1 beaten egg

1 10½-ounce can condensed French onion soup

2 cups herb-seasoned stuffing mix

½ teaspoon seasoned salt

2 pounds ground beef

1 cup salsa-style catsup or regular catsup

1 8-ounce can tomato sauce

1 cup water

⅓ cup packed brown sugar

¼ cup Worcestershire sauce

¼ cup vinegar

2 tablespoons quick-cooking tapioca

In a large bowl combine egg, soup, stuffing mix, and salt. Add ground beef; mix well. Shape into 1-inch meatballs. Place meatballs in a 15×10×1-inch baking pan. Bake in a 350° oven for 15 to 18 minutes or until no pink remains in centers of meatballs. Drain meatballs and transfer to a 3½-, 4-, or 5-quart crockery cooker.

In a medium bowl combine catsup, tomato sauce, water, brown sugar, Worcestershire sauce, vinegar, and tapioca. Pour over meatballs; stir gently to coat.

Cover; cook on high-heat setting for 2 to 3 hours. Serve immediately or keep warm on low-heat setting for up to 2 hours. Serve with toothpicks. Makes about 50 meatballs.

Nutrition facts per meatball: 58 calories, 4 g protein, 5 g carbohydrate, 3 g total fat (1 g saturated), 15 mg cholesterol, 191 mg sodium

sweet 'n' sour hamballs

1 9- or 10-ounce bottle sweet
and sour sauce

⅓ cup unsweetened pineapple juice

⅓ cup packed brown sugar

¼ teaspoon ground ginger

1 beaten egg

½ cup graham cracker crumbs

2 tablespoons milk

½ pound ground cooked ham

½ pound ground pork

Nonstick spray coating

In a 3½- or 4-quart crockery cooker stir together sweet and sour sauce, pineapple juice, brown sugar, and ground ginger. Set aside.

For meatballs, in a large bowl combine egg, graham cracker crumbs, and milk. Add ground ham and pork; mix well. Shape into 30 meatballs. Spray a 12-inch skillet with nonstick coating. Add meatballs and brown on all sides over medium heat.

Add meatballs to crockery cooker. Stir to coat. Cover; cook on low-heat setting for 4 to 5 hours or on high-heat setting for 1½ to 2 hours. Serve immediately or keep warm on low-heat setting for up to 2 hours. Makes 30 meatballs.

Nutrition facts per meatball: 51 calories, 3 g protein, 7 g carbohydrate, 1g total fat (0 g saturated), 13 mg cholesterol, 130 mg sodium

sausage bites

1½ cups bottled barbecue sauce

⅔ cup orange marmalade

½ teaspoon dry mustard

⅛ teaspoon ground allspice

¾ pound fully cooked bratwurst, cut into ½-inch-thick slices

¾ pound fully cooked kielbasa, cut diagonally into ½-inch-thick slices

½ pound small fully cooked smoked sausage links

1 8-ounce can pineapple chunks, drained

In a 3½- or 4-quart crockery cooker combine barbecue sauce, orange marmalade, dry mustard, and allspice. Stir in bratwurst, kielbasa, and smoked sausage links.

Cover; cook on high-heat setting for 2½ to 3 hours. Stir in pineapple chunks. Serve immediately or keep warm on the low-heat setting for up to 2 hours. Makes 20 servings.

Nutrition facts per serving: 198 calories, 7 g protein, 12 g carbohydrate, 13 g total fat (5 g saturated), 32 mg cholesterol, 578 mg sodium

tips from the kitchen

putting cooking on hold Have there ever been times when you were concerned about not returning home until well after your crockery cooker recipe was finished? There's an easy remedy: Use an automatic timer, purchased at a hardware store, to start the cooker. When using a timer, be sure all ingredients are well-chilled when you place them in the cooker. Never use this method with frozen fish or poultry. Also, the food should not stand for longer than 2 hours before cooking begins.

supreme pizza fondue

Your finicky family will love this spin on one of their favorite foods. Serve this pizza-flavored fondue for a graduation party or a birthday party. (Recipe pictured on page 84.)

4 ounces bulk Italian sausage

1 small onion, finely chopped

1 clove garlic, minced

1 30-ounce jar meatless spaghetti sauce

1 cup sliced fresh mushrooms

2/3 cup chopped pepperoni or Canadian-style bacon

1 teaspoon dried basil or oregano, crushed

1/2 cup sliced pitted ripe olives (optional)

1/4 cup chopped green sweet pepper (optional)

Dippers, such as focaccia bread or Italian bread cubes, mozzarella or provolone cheese cubes, or cooked tortellini or ravioli

In a large skillet cook the sausage, onion, and garlic until meat is brown. Drain off fat.

In a 3½- or 4-quart crockery cooker combine spaghetti sauce, mushrooms, pepperoni or Canadian-style bacon, and basil or oregano. Stir in the meat mixture.

Cover; cook on low-heat setting for 3 hours. If desired, stir in ripe olives and sweet pepper. Cover; cook on low-heat setting for 15 minutes. To serve, spear the dippers with fondue forks and dip into the fondue. Makes 10 servings (about 5½ cups).

Nutrition facts per serving (with cheese and tortellini dippers): 254 calories, 13 g protein, 24 g carbohydrate, 12 g total fat (4 g saturated), 39 mg cholesterol, 738 mg sodium

mulled cranberry cider

With a libation like this, your guests may not want to leave the party. It's a great starter for a dinner, a brunch, or a simple evening of appetizers and good cheer.

1 small orange

8 cups cranberry-raspberry drink

¼ cup packed brown sugar

6 inches stick cinnamon

3 star anise

1 teaspoon whole cloves

Orange peel strips (optional)

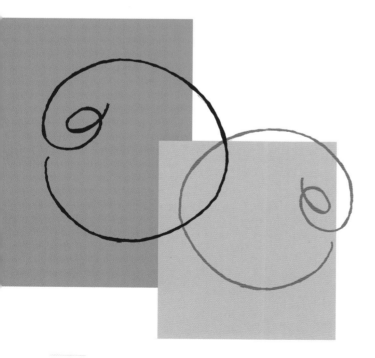

Remove the orange portion of the orange peel using a vegetable peeler. Cut peel into strips. Squeeze juice from orange; discard seeds and pulp. In a 3½-, 4-, or 5-quart crockery cooker combine orange juice, cranberry-raspberry drink, and brown sugar.

For spice bag, cut a double thickness of 100 percent cotton cheesecloth into an 8-inch square. Place the orange peel, cinnamon, star anise, and whole cloves in center of cheesecloth square. Bring corners of cheesecloth together and tie with a clean cotton string. Add to crockery cooker.

Cover; cook on low-heat setting for 5 to 6 hours or on high-heat setting for 2½ to 3 hours. To serve, remove the spice bag and discard. Ladle cider into cups. If desired, garnish with additional orange peel. Makes 10 (6-ounce) servings.

Nutrition facts per serving: 152 calories, 0 g protein, 37 g carbohydrate, 0 g total fat, 0 mg cholesterol, 30 mg sodium

mulled wine

Since boiling wine makes it bitter, the crockery cooker is a great way to warm this classic drink.

2 whole cardamom pods

16 whole cloves

3 inches stick cinnamon, broken

2 750-milliliter bottles dry red wine

2 cups water

1 cup light-colored corn syrup

2 oranges, halved

Orange slices, halved (optional)

Cinnamon sticks (optional)

For spice bag, cut a double thickness of 100 percent cotton cheesecloth into a 5- or 6-inch square. Pinch cardamom pods to break open. Place cardamom, cloves, and the 3 inches stick cinnamon in center of cheesecloth square. Bring corners of cheesecloth together and tie with a clean cotton string.

In a 3½-, 4-, or 5-quart crockery cooker combine wine, water, and corn syrup. Add spice bag.

Cover; cook on low-heat setting for 4 to 5 hours or on high-heat setting for 2 to 2½ hours. (Do not let boil.)

Add orange halves the last ½ hour of cooking. Remove spice bag and orange halves and discard.

To serve, ladle beverage into cups. If desired, float a fresh orange slice half on top of each serving and add a cinnamon stick. Makes 12 (6-ounce) servings.

Nutrition facts per serving: 180 calories, 1 g protein, 25 g carbohydrate, 0 g total fat, 0 mg cholesterol, 102 mg sodium

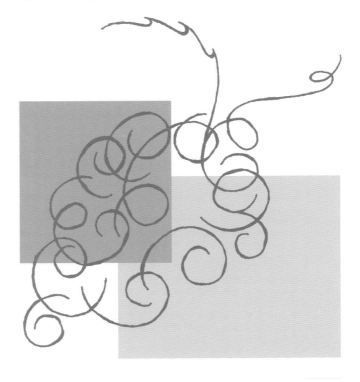

chocolate cream cocoa

Vary this rich and delicious drink by using different flavored creamers and liqueurs.

1 9.6-ounce package nonfat dry milk powder (about 3½ cups)

¾ cup powdered sugar

¾ cup unsweetened cocoa powder

¾ cup Irish cream-flavored powdered nondairy creamer or plain powdered nondairy creamer

8 cups water

½ cup crème de cacao (optional)

Sweetened whipped cream

In a 3½-, 4-, or 5-quart crockery cooker combine dry milk powder, powdered sugar, cocoa powder, and nondairy creamer. Gradually add water; stir well to dissolve.

Cover; cook on low-heat setting for 3 to 4 hours or on high-heat setting for 1½ to 2 hours.

If desired, stir in the crème de cacao. Stir mixture before serving. Ladle into mugs; top with whipped cream. Makes about 12 (6-ounce) servings.

Nutrition facts per serving: 214 calories, 9 g protein, 30 g carbohydrate, 7 g total fat (5 g saturated), 14 mg cholesterol, 147 mg sodium

tips from the kitchen

beverages at the ready When it's cold and damp outside, greet your guests with the enticing aroma of a beverage simmering in your crockery cooker (see recipes, pages 92 to 94). On the low-heat setting, your hot beverage will stay a perfect sipping temperature throughout the party. And because your guests can serve themselves from the cooker, you will save on replenishing trips back and forth to the range-top.

index